ADAPT AND OVERCOME

What Business Owners Need to Do to Keep Employees, Clients and Infrastructure Safe During a Time of Crisis

Prominence Publishing
www.prominencepublishing.com

Adapt and Overcome/Chris Wiser. -- 1st ed.
ISBN: 978-1-988925-61-5

Contents

Foreword

By Chris Wiser

This year has brought an uncertainty to business owners that has wreaked havoc in the business community across the world. The world we once knew has been forever changed and businesses in all different industries have been negatively impacted by what has been the most catastrophic crisis of the decade.

2020 has presented a typhoon of uncertainties that has threatened most business owners worldwide. Entrepreneurs around the world are having to adapt and change the way they have been doing business for years. Through this period, I have learned much about my own business that I had not realized before: it takes planning, strategy, and dedication to ensure my business longevity.

Constant implementation and execution allowed my business to continue to grow and prosper in recent months. Not to mention, I had taken steps prior to this crisis that would ensure I could continue to grow my business, given the worldwide health and economic crisis that affected much of the world. For example, maintaining a business continuity and disaster recovery plan ensured that I could continue to grow my business through the business shutdowns, economic turmoil and uncertainty this crisis had brought to our communities. It also helps that I have a business model that can support a completely remote working environment. All of my employees live in different parts of the world.

Even through the burdens that came along with this crisis, business planning and disaster recovery helped ensure that my business would continue to run smoothly going through, and coming out of, these uncertain times. Most of the world has been hit extremely hard this year with what is known as the Coronavirus pandemic, which has wreaked havoc on the business community as a whole. Due to the pandemic, nonessential businesses have been required to shut their doors, only able to continue business remotely, without the availability of an office for their employees. As most of us understand, some business models cannot achieve a remote working model as they require an actual building to produce specific products and/or services. For example, fitness facilities, manufacturing plants, hair and nail salons, and many other businesses are simply unable to sustain a remote working model. These types of businesses have been hit the hardest. However, if your business can support a remote working model, it is important that you have a plan in place for your business to sustain the next bought of uncertain times.

For most of the business community, the economic impact of this period has been devastating. Having a business that is able to accommodate a remote working model allows your employees to continue doing their jobs from the comfort of their own homes. Although some businesses are able to accommodate staff that can work from home, most businesses don't know the correct process to go about properly adapting and securing employees that work from home. Most business owners are not concerning themselves with how their remotely working employees are securing their business assets and confidential data, which is a huge concern of mine when I think about the growing number of businesses that now support remote employees. Not properly securing your business network leaves your confidential information and business assets at risk. During a time of crisis, it is easy for business owners to take the easy way out to secure business longevity instead of taking the necessary steps to securing their assets.

How are you making sure your business assets are being secured with a remote workforce? Since you cannot be looking over their shoulder at all times, it is important to ensure your business network is secure from hackers and your employees are knowledgeable and educated about stopping hacking attempts to steal your business assets, money or personal data.

The most unfortunate fact about cybersecurity is that while most businesses NEED to protect their business, most are not WILLING to take on the extra cost of protecting their business from hackers. The war against hackers has only begun, and as more and more businesses migrate to a remote working model, the more opportunity there is for hackers. Hackers are able to expunge data, acquire confidential information and steal money.

The severity of hacking has become a reality for most business owners around the world and as these uncertain times drag on, more hackers are seeing the true opportunity for hacking your network. The repercussions of a cyber attack are catastrophic and at the very worst, could cause you your business. That is why we have brought a group of expert business owners together to discuss how your business can survive the next uncertain times and secure longevity through the next crisis.

Chris Wiser,

CEO, 7 Figure MSP

Speaker/Trainer/
Entrepreneur Coach

How a Crisis Can Affect Your Business

By Steve Schabacker

Living in the 21st century, we take things for granted in many areas of our life. This can be anything from our job to our family or friends. As a business owner, we often have many more things to take for granted, especially if the business has been around for many years and is doing well. It is easy to put things on cruise control and start to feel invincible. This is a very dangerous place to be, regardless of what industry you are in. A crisis can come out of nowhere, without any warning, and attack your business. Do you think you are safe?

Allow me to share the story of a business owner who was recently in this position. For the purposes of this story, we will call him John. John is one of the physician owners of a clinic serving all ages of clients with family practice services. Over the years, the practice has grown and done very well. He is well known in the area and had been consistently growing in the twenty-one years the practice has existed. Things were going well for John and the practice until the unexpected happened, a pandemic followed by a ransomware attack on his practice.

Could John have expected the pandemic and been fully prepared? Most likely not. When it hit, he tried to move as rapidly as possible and have what staff could work from home. This was a bit of an undertaking in itself as John had always opted for the cheapest options in IT infrastructure and support. He figured 'good enough was good enough' and there was no reason to spend money on anything better. This created some big headaches when trying to move staff home and still have them able to work effectively. John learned he was not prepared for any of this and it would be very costly. Unfortunately, at this point he had no choice and no time to explore options.

Just as the dust was settling on the operational changes, things got much worse. His network had been infected by ransomware and he could not access any of his patient files, test results, imaging, or billing records. He was locked out of everything. He did not realize how catastrophic this was until contacting his IT support company. After seeing the lockout message, he assumed a reboot or something of that nature would fix everything. John was in for a big surprise. You see, John cut corners on IT. He avoided wasting money on offsite backups and other luxuries like cyber security protection.

Stopped dead in his tracks, John had to shut down operation of his practice. Without access to patient charts, billing, and test results, he could not see patients. He brought in his IT support company, but it was not much help. They really just specialized in setting up hardware and printers and were out of their element. After a couple of days of searching, John found ransomware experts to bring in. They confirmed the worst – he had no choice but to pay the ransom. Without backups, there was no choice. John then proceeded to send the $250,000 in Bitcoin the ransom demanded. It was more cash than he had available, but he was able to pull from personal saving to get it done. The ransom promised once the money was verified, a code to unencrypt the files would be sent.

A day passed, then two and finally a week went by without any communication from the hackers. Now not only was John's practice shut down, but he was also out a large sum of money and still locked out of everything. The nightmare would not stop. John proceeded to find a company to wipe and rebuild all of his systems and get him back up and running. The price was even bigger than what he had already paid the hackers and the process would not be quick. He was already dealing with upset patients who needed care, staff that needed to work, and no access to anything.

John's options were grim. There was no easy or cheap way out. John's legacy was all hanging there in the balance. After much deliberation, John decided to shut down his practice. This put 38 staff members out of work, over 3,000 patients looking for a new primary care doctor, and John looking for a job elsewhere. Twenty-one years of John's blood, sweat, and tears went into this practice that was lost because of some poor decisions and cutting corners. His legacy that he hoped would outlive him was gone in an instant. Unfortunately, John's story is just one of many I could share.

The first question I always get after telling this story is *"Could what happened to John have been avoided?"* The answer is yes, and I will spend the rest of this chapter discussing the types of problems that a crisis can cause to your business, as well as best practices to avoid them. Like so many things in life, the answers are simple but not easy.

Things such as what industry you are in, how long you have been in business, or even the size of your business are often irrelevant in this discussion of defending your business. The problems we see typically arise from the neglect in one of the key areas of focus, which I call the **4 Ps: Partners, Planning, Protection,** and **Practice.** These 4 areas are all inter-related and without all four there are holes that could allow a catastrophic event to be fatal on your business.

Partners – This is the first P and arguably the most important. In this case, the partner would be an IT company (or possibly multiple companies) that would partner with your business to become an extension of your team. They are more than simply a vendor as the integration needs to be very tight.

The role they serve is that of chief information officer and their team below. Selecting the right partner is very important. It needs to be a firm you trust and in which you have full confidence. In today's world, a normal IT company will not be acceptable. You must find a partner that specializes in cyber security first and foremost, as that is the most difficult piece to the puzzle. Any IT provider can manage your computers, install printers, and maintain your network, but most do not have cyber security expertise. Once you find the right partner, you can move on to the other Ps.

Planning – Simply having a partner is not enough. The first thing you need to do is engage that partner in helping you come up with a plan. This plan will include all of the "What Ifs" that could cause your business harm and how those risks can be addressed. These should include situations such as hacks, breaches, rogue employees, acts of God, hardware failure, and other scenarios. Without thinking about and working through responses to each of these issues, it is impossible to react effectively when one occurs. It is not a matter of if your business will be affected by one of these, but simply a matter of when. Having a plan will save you money and could even save your business.

Protection – Once you have a partner and create a plan, they must then put the appropriate protections in place. These protections are what we would call a cyber security stack. The stack is basically a group of tools and processes that work together to provide layers of defense for your systems. The easiest way to explain this is thinking of a castle. All castles are unique, but they often have similar defense that all layer with one another to provide the most protection possible. For example, castles often have a moat, walls, and a drawbridge. By combining these, the protection is increased. The moat keeps people from reaching the walls when the drawbridge is up. The drawbridge also doubles as a barrier, also keeping people out should they get past the moat. Add on some towers with archers and that adds more security. Each layer serves a purpose itself, but when combined with other layers they are each even more effective.

Practice – With a partner in place, a plan created, and now protection in place, the last item is practice. Just as any sports team does not just go out and play a game, you cannot depend on your plans to work if they are never practiced. Running mock scenarios provides practice for the team that would be deploying your plans in an emergency. One of the most important plans involves how to restore your systems from a backup and get your business running after an event. Practicing will make sure there are no snags in the plan, nothing has been missed, and that your business is operational again as quickly as possible.

All of this can be summed up into one additional P word – **Preparation**. As a business owner, you need to be ready for the expected challenges that come your way, as well as the unexpected ones that you could never expect to happen to your business. The way I like to explain it is pretty simple, do you want to play checkers or chess? While the games are played on the same board, they are nothing alike. In the game of checkers, there are only so many possible moves and the variations are quite simple, and most players are only looking a move or two ahead of it all. In the game of chess, you must be thinking far ahead and anticipating what you opponent is going to do. Without strategizing and anticipating your opponent, you will likely lose. Protecting your business is no different.

If you are currently playing checkers but want to transition into playing chess, we can help you. Before that can happen, however, you must first figure out exactly where you are right now as well as where you need to be. Starting that process is just a click away. Go to wesecureinc.com and make an appointment for a complimentary 30-minute consultation with me or one of my team. We would be happy to help in any way we can.

I'm often asked why I am so passionate about helping small businesses protect themselves. The answer is simple: I don't want to see another small business go through what so many have. I will leave you with one simple request: talk to someone and find out exactly what position your business is in. By someone, I don't mean your copier company that also does IT support. Find an expert in cybersecurity who can give you an expert opinion on the current security state and preparedness of your business. Then at least you know and, as GI Joe used to say, "knowing is half of the battle."

About the Author

Steve Schabacker is CEO and co-founder of We Secure Cyber Security, a Cyber Security and IT Support provider. Steve brings to the table 26 years of experience in the IT industry, holding many different positions over the years in various organizations. His diversified experience allows him a unique perspective and the ability to view problems in a holistic manner.

Steve's team at We Secure take great pride in helping businesses stay safe and secure while supporting all of their IT needs.

You can connect with Steve online at https://www.linkedin.com/in/steve-schabacker and connect with We Secure at https://www.facebook.com/wesecureinc

Crisis Management During a Business Downturn

By Jeri Morgan

Kelly is the owner of a small CPA firm with 20 employees. Her business had grown from 1 employee to 20 in the span of two years. With the quick growth, Kelly never had taken the time to do any disaster or crisis planning for her business. She utilized technology in her business but did not necessarily look at ways in which technology could change her business. It had a PBX phone system, an onsite server, and in general a business that was set up for all work to be done onsite in the office. She did not believe in staff members being able to work from home and certainly had not set up her business in a way that allowed for remote work to occur.

When the Covid-19 crisis hit right in the middle of tax season, Kelly and her business were thrown for a loop. In short order, she was scrambling to figure out how her business could keep serving her clients remotely. She was desperate, too, for revenue to be able to come into her business and to keep her staff employed.

The problems: they had an inflexible phone system that did not have the ability to move with them, they had data stored in a way staff couldn't access it, and a lot of their records were still stored on paper in the office. They needed to be agile, but they were figuratively and literally stuck.

This was an emergency. Kelly called my company in a panic. We talked with her at length about her business, her staff, and her current setup. She needed to move... and move quickly. This was crisis management in action. We had to figure out what they needed and get it implemented as soon as possible. We put a phone system in place that was literally plug and play. She could send her employees home with a phone that they could plug in when they got home and had the ability to take customer calls and transfer to other staff members as well. We set up all the employees' computers securely to be able to log into the server from home and complete their jobs effectively and efficiently. We made sure that we had security measures in place at each employee's home to protect the sensitive customer data with which they were working. We set them up with some great cloud-based communication tools so they could keep in contact with each other and collaborate just as they had been able to when they were 5 feet from one another.

Odds are when you made the decision to start your business, the words 'crisis management' never entered your mind. You were an expert at something. You had a gift that you wanted to share with the world. As time went on, the business grew, and you began to add to your team. With scaling your business, the number of hats that you had to manage grew as well.

In the day-to-day running of your business, crisis management just did not make the top of your to-do list. As many businesses have found when faced with a crisis for which we do not plan, we most certainly will fail. Period.

What is Crisis Management?

At its core, crisis management is simple. It is simply the process with which we can plan for emergency or disruptive events that could affect your ability to do business. These disruptive events can be natural disasters (fire, earthquake, flood), a community crisis (pandemic, civil unrest), technological (cyber-attacks, hardware failure), or business (loss of large client, vendor closes doors).

As you can see, even though we typically think of natural disasters when we talk about a crisis, all businesses need to consider the other types that can and will occur over the life of a long-standing business. None of us want to think about a crisis, an economic downturn, or a rough patch for our business. Strong businesses, businesses that survive the test of time, have one thing in common: risk management.

Your business will face rough times, things that are outside of your control, things that can close your doors. If you make plans to manage the risk and are proactive in protecting your company, you not only can survive, but thrive during a crisis.

8 Things You Can Do Now to Protect Your Company During a Business Downturn

Create a Plan. Take the time to create a concise, well-defined plan for your business. Identify objectives. The plan should address how to protect employees and the company itself during a crisis, how communication will occur (both to staff and to clients), and a step-by-step action plan of exactly what will be done and who will do it during a crisis. It is important in this preplanning stage to identify what team member will be the communications representative and what team member will be the operations representative ensuring that the plan is followed.

Take Care of Your Team. The success or failure in any business lays in their team. Take the time carefully to cultivate a strong team and a team that can support the vision that you have for the organization. During a crisis, the first thing that people often go to is layoffs. Slow down. Take a moment to consider how you can take care of your team. Perhaps a situation where each team member has an extra day off per week unpaid or the entire team takes a small pay cut in order to keep the team intact. Communicate with your staff, find out what it is are willing to do. If you take care of your team, many times it will take care of you.

Cash is King. We have all heard that old saying that cash is king and most definitely during a crisis this holds true. There is no worse feeling in the middle of a crisis than to keep your eyes on a dwindling bank account. Build up an emergency fund that is going to cover all expenses for your business plus some for 6-9 months. We always hear about individuals who are living paycheck to paycheck. A lesser known fact is how many businesses in our own communities are being run the same way. Before you find yourself in a crisis, take some CFO time for your business. Truthfully examine your revenue and your expenses. If your expenses are out of line, it is time either to increase your revenue, cut some unneeded expenses, or some combination of both.

Credit Utilization. It is much easier to obtain credit before you need it. In crisis after crisis, we have seen businesses rushing to find credit, bank loans, grants, to try and keep their businesses open. The problem is that during a crisis, money can be hard to find. The best time to seek credit is when you do not need it; when the economy is flying high, when you have more money coming into your business than you know what to do with. This is the time to apply for credit. Establish relationships with multiple financial institutions, local community banks and credit unions are historically best for small businesses. Once you establish credit, use it but pay it off every month. Keep the balances low and available in case there is a crisis in which you need to it.

Grade Your Customers and Your Products. When times are good, as business owners we can tend to grow our product offering to a size that is not always manageable. Additionally, we may have added clients that are not particularly profitable. Look at both your offerings and your clients. Invest your organization's time and energy in those products and customers that are most profitable. This does require a thorough analysis to ensure that all the costs are being considered and the picture being provided is accurate. Once that is done, you may make the decision to do some pruning that will allow your organization once again to grow.

Recurring Revenue. Create a business model in which you are supporting clients through ongoing monthly service agreements. On the one hand, it is going to lend itself to supporting your clients in a more robust way, creating an all-around better experience for your clients. Additionally, it is going to create predictable revenue for your business month in and month out. You can certainly create opportunities to do special projects for your clients. However, in the event of a crisis or an economic downturn, having predictable monthly revenue will allow you to weather the storm much easier than a business that is solely driven by one-off or project work.

Be in It to Win It. Go on the offense. During a crisis, many companies will be frozen in fear, afraid to make any changes, afraid to market, afraid to make a move at all. Do what everyone else is not doing and make investments in your business. Do not cut back on marketing, this is the time you need to be marketing. Pay attention to new market opportunities, pivot and be ready to strategically position yourself directly where competitors are not.

Technology. Evaluate the technology that your organization is using often. This is one area where it is extremely difficult to make changes in mid crisis. Utilize, at a minimum, an outsourced IT Company; one that offers a fractional CTO may be a good idea. Rely on their expertise to guide the technological direction you should take. They can help your organization create more productivity within your organization. They can help to guide both your security and the agility of your organization. If there is one thing that we have learned in recent years, it is the importance of flexibility: working from the office, remotely, using cloud solutions, social media. From a technological perspective, the rate at which you adopt and adapt to change may be the difference between being in business or being out of business.

Crisis management will be one of the most important exercises that you delve into as a business owner. It is important to remember that this is certainly not a once-and-done type of situation. As a business owner, it is important to take a good look at your crisis management plan at least yearly. If you can do that, when you find yourself staring directly at a crisis you will be calm, you will be ready, and you will be successful.

(Q

You can book a 30-minute free strategy session with Jeri by emailing her at: jerim@codebluecomputing.com.

About the Author

Jeri Morgan is the President of Code Blue Computing headquartered in Denver, Colorado. Code Blue Computing is a Security First organization specializing in Cyber Security, IT Consulting, and Cloud Services. Code Blue Computing was named the 2012 Small Business of the Year by the City of Thornton, Colorado and the 2014 Emerging Business of the Year by The Broomfield Chamber of Commerce. Jeri was nominated for the Denver Business Journal Outstanding Women in Business Award in 2016 and in 2019.

A common-sense leader with a multi-faceted background in Manufacturing, Operations, and

Logistics, Jeri has a knack for meeting Business Owners exactly where they are to help them build best business practices as it relates to security and utilizing technology to improve their bottom line.

Code Blue Computing

Phone: 720-746-9763

jeri@codebluecomputing.com

http://codebluecomputing.com

Preventing Cyber Attacks When Business is in Jeopardy

By Bryan M Hornung

Just a couple of weeks ago we had some severe early summer storms blow through our area, causing widespread power and internet outages. When I returned home from the office, the power was out. The electric company posted online that we would have power restored within 2 days. The power rarely went out for an extended period of time at my home in which I've lived for just over 3 years. I had a feeling that this time we might be without power for some time. I was fairly certain it was time to bust out the generator that I had yet to use in our new home. The thought of digging the generator out of the detached garage was not something I was really relishing. I also had not attempted to start said generator in over 3 years. Knowing this, I told my wife I'll wait until 7 PM before I even think about using the generator.

It was 7 PM before I knew it, and a few minutes later in the heat and humidity, there I was digging through miter saws, bikes, quads, and you name it, to get to the generator that was buried somewhere in the middle of the 24' long garage. Once I finally had the generator out of the garage, I faced my next challenge: firing up a machine I have not even laid eyes on in nearly 3 years.

The generator was half full of gasoline, which was probably stale, but I wasn't about to empty it as it was nearly half full. I checked the oil level, which was surprisingly OK, and turned on the fuel valve and give a few pulls on the starter ... and nothing. In the distance, I can hear my neighbor's dedicated generator purring away as I stare at the lights on inside their home. I recalled the time my neighbor told me he was putting one in several years ago because he wanted his family to have power with the flip of a switch, due to the fact that he traveled for work often. He just didn't want the stress of being away and not being able to help his family.

I continued on, trying to get my generator started. After about 20-30 minutes of fussing with different levers and switches (and about 50 pulls on the starter), I found it odd I did not see an engine choke. After staring at the machine for about 5, maybe 10 minutes, and convincing myself I had to be missing a choke I suddenly found it. A small black lever hidden right behind the air filter. Eureka! Slide the lever to full choke, one pull and... Viola! We have power and Dad saved the day!

About 10 minutes after I get the generator started, our other neighbor (across the way) called and asked if we knew where he can get a generator. They called everywhere, and no one had them. I just replied, "This is probably the worst time to buy a generator, they don't last long when the power is out."

I look at my situation with the storm and can't help to draw a correlation between those events and how I see many businesses are prepared for disaster. There are leaders who are very good at preparing for events before they happen; there are leaders who are good at reacting to events. Hopefully, through learned experience, they will be more prepared to deal with the same issues if they happen in the future. Then we have the others who choose to do nothing and deal with the consequences of the events as they unfold before their very eyes.

Just like the storm I went through, a cyberattack can wreak havoc on your business at any time. The attackers behind a cyberattack do not care about your bankruptcy, that your store just got looted, or that your business was shut down due to a global pandemic. Cyber thieves are opportunists and look for every opportunity to prey on humans when they are at their weakest. They are no different than any other criminal, except they are usually faceless and can operate at all hours of the day, going mostly undetected, from anywhere in the world.

The unfortunate fact about a business in crisis mode is that the weak points of the company's processes and procedures along with the blind spots of the leaders end up having a big bright spotlight shined right on the problems. It makes the littlest problems seem a million times bigger, and a lot more expensive to fix. The real answer to how a business prevents a cyberattack when the business itself is facing more than one challenge is this: Start planning. Now.

My hope is that when you read this, you will start to take necessary steps, today, to begin planning for a cyberattack or any event that could adversely affect your business operations.

Let's pretend for a minute you weren't like my neighbor with the dedicated generator. Let's say you are more like me, or my neighbor across the way with no generator. What can a business do to prevent a cyberattack when their business is faced with challenges? In the spring of 2020, we saw a lot of businesses faced with this exact scenario. Businesses all over the U.S. were struggling to deal with the restrictions placed on them as a result of government trying to control the spread of COVID-19. On top of that, many businesses in major cities across the U.S. had to deal with looting and losses as a result of social injustice demonstrations. How can a business protect itself when faced with events that no one really ever expected to be facing?

I am going to outline the 5 Steps that I recommend every business use to create and refine their disaster recovery plan. Developing the plan and committing it to writing can be done at very little cost if you do it yourself. You can also seek outside professionals to help you with some or all of the plan. Over time, you will want to invest in and expand on the disaster recovery plan, but if you run a small company and funds are tight, you can start by doing it yourself. Here's what to do.

Step 1 - Identify

The first thing businesses need to do is identify the systems and data they absolutely need to remain operational. Businesses should designate systems and data with 3 distinct labels: Critical, essential, and non-essential. Critical systems would be the systems your business absolutely needs to operate and cannot run without. Essential functions are the systems and data the you may need but could do without for a period without impacting normal operations or revenue. Finally, non-essential systems are systems that the business could function without for an extended period of time.

Once you have gone through and identified and, more importantly, documented the importance of systems and data in your business, you can then move on to the next step of protecting those things you identified.

Step 2 - Protect

Protecting your business' computer system doesn't simply mean putting antivirus software on the computers and servers you own. This is a common misconception among business owners. Protect means protecting the business more than it means protecting data or systems. To do this, business leaders should take the systems and data identified in Step 1 and define two critical benchmarks:

First, how long can that data or system be unavailable before it negatively impacts revenue?

Second, how far back in time can we go should we need to recover before it negatively impacts revenue?

Knowing these two benchmarks will give you the answer to which technologies and options are available to you in order to achieve your business goals and reduce your risk should you need to move into a recovery operation. The general rule, though, is that the less time your business can operate without real time data or the systems being available, the higher the costs will be to protect them. This is why it is critical to define the importance of these systems so your business can assess risk should the systems or data become unavailable. You can then put a price tag on how much it's "worth" to invest in a backup and recovery system that is in line with your business goals. The Protect step is where you decide whether you need an automatic failover generator, the manual start generator in the shed, or no generator at all.

Step 3 – Detect

When it comes to disaster recovery, in almost every case, the faster you detect you have a problem the less damage that occurs as a result of the event. This is true with both natural disasters and cyberattacks. Knowing and acknowledging you have the problem is half the battle. Finding out your systems were infected with ransomware at 8 PM Friday evening on the following Monday morning is less than ideal. Finding out while the event is occurring is the most ideal. Both scenarios are entirely possible with the technology we have today, so are the outcomes from such events.

Just like my neighbor who has the automatic power-loss detection, you can choose to have detection and alerting in real time. You can also wait until disaster strikes, like my neighbor across the way, and discover you are unable to get the help and resource you need when you need it most (this is usually the most expensive). You can even have something in between, like my trusty garage-stored generator. You get to decide how much risk you want to tolerate in your business. Just be sure to work with a professional who can advise you on the pros and cons of your decisions or taking on certain levels of risk.

Step 4 – Respond

Once you have detected a cyberattack – it's time to respond. Responding can mean a lot of different things to a lot of different businesses. I am going to cover how all businesses should handle responding to a cyberattack at a very high level. Your state and local laws, as well as any regulations, compliance, or contracts, and agreements, may also dictate how you can and should respond to a cyberattack. Always consult a professional.

That being said, your business' response is predicated on you having the previous 4 steps documented and adopted as policy. Your response may be dictated or influenced by your cyber-insurance policy, or a client or vendor's contracts. Therefore, it is important that you identify these requirements in Step 1.

The next part of responding is putting the plan into action. It is also a good idea to engage experts – IT professionals, lawyers, and insurance agents at this point if you have been attempting to go at this alone or with someone who is not qualified. The response step will be the key to your roadmap to recovery and getting back to business quickly, or going out of business. The outcome a business has when it responds to a cyberattack is a direct result of the time and money invested in the 5-step plan as I have laid out here, along with testing and improving it regularly.

If you want to make your response step a successful one, then you must test it. Knowing how to respond, and conducting live disaster recovery testing or "fire drills" will not only ensure future success and reduce stress on you and your team. It will also give you the information you need to allow your business to identify gaps in your overall response plan and will greatly improve the success of this step. The last thing you want to do is implement your recovery for the first time under a real disaster event.

Step 5 – Recover

Getting business back to "normal" is the goal of this step. There are many options depending on your situation when it comes to recovering your business. Unfortunately, many businesses don't make it to this step; and if they do, this is the step they get only to die a painfully slow death. Some 25% of all small businesses fail after a cyberattack. That number goes up even higher when a business is in the midst of dealing with other business-impacting events like natural disasters. In my experience, the businesses that make it to this step and go on to resume normal operations have successfully implemented the 4 other steps and refined and improved upon them regularly upon testing. You are significantly increasing your chances of total business failure if you are not doing disaster recovery testing in your business.

The 5 Steps I laid out above are a high-level overview of what every business leader needs to consider if they want to get through a cyberattack.

This applies in good times and when businesses are faced with challenges outside of their control. There are a couple of additional points I want to raise that are critical and a lot of businesses make these mistakes, so I feel it is important to mention.

First, document, document, document. The entire plan needs to be written down so anyone with basic computer knowledge can pick it up and understand it. Far too many businesses allow one person to handle the recovery plan and many times don't even write it down. When you are in the midst of a crisis, or multiple crises, having to recall your disaster recovery plan from memory usually doesn't lead to a successful recovery. Plus, not having your plan documented is a sure-fire way to have your cyber-insurance claim outright denied, let alone forgetting the simple things like I did when I was unable to locate the choke when I needed to get my generator started.

It is also a huge risk to your business to have your disaster recovery plan with only one person. Cybersecurity and disaster recovery are components in a team sport, and should be treated as such. The more you make planning and recovery part of your culture, the more people you will have helping you get back to normal.

Second, the more you invest in planning and prevention, the less time, money, and resources you will need to spend on remediation and recovery. "An ounce of prevention is worth a pound of cure" certainly applies here. The time to plan is now. External events you cannot control, already being in the midst of a crisis – these are not excuses to procrastinate. Your clients, employees, partners, and vendors depend on you to open your doors every day. If you have never thought about how your business would recover from one or multiple events, start today.

Every CEO and business leader needs to know there are many tools and resources available to you to solve these problems and help you implement your own 5-step plan. One of the easiest ways is to hire a Managed Service Provider who offers compliance and cybersecurity services. These MSPs are already equipped with the tools and expertise your business needs to survive natural disasters and cyberattacks.

No matter how you go about it, the real question is how much risk and stress can you or your business tolerate? Will you be like my neighbors across the way who lost all their food and had no power for days? Or will you be semi-prepared like I was and run around scrambling trying to remember how to get vaguely familiar systems up and running? Or will you be like my next-door neighbor who simply walked into his garage and flipped a switch and went on with his day? It really all depends on how much time and money you invest in what is required to do ahead of time for the day you need to put the plan into action.

About the Author

Bryan Hornung is CEO/President of Xact IT Solutions. He has consulted with and helped hundreds of businesses demystify technology since starting Xact IT Solutions in 2004.

Bryan's career began in 1999 as a consultant for the NAVSEA's Naval Surface Warfare Center, Carderock Division (NSWCCD), where he was instrumental in implementing web-based technologies to help coordinate projects between engineers and the U.S. Navy fleet. His work earned him the opportunity to work closely with naval captains and their civil counterparts, arming him with the confidence and knowledge to start his own business.

His excellent reputation at NAVSEA paved the way for many key opportunities and he began moonlighting as an IT consultant for a few small businesses while still employed as a DoD contractor. A couple years later, he grew his moonlighting opportunities into a full-time consulting and I.T. business and officially started Xact IT Solutions Inc.

As CEO, Bryan oversees the daily operations of the company while also consulting with C-Level clients and business owners as a CIO for their businesses. Bryan's focus is always on making sure his clients receive the best service possible by constantly helping them improve efficiency and their profitability through the use of technology and the right services. This dedication to his clients has been recognized throughout the years; Xact IT Solutions has won multiple awards for outstanding customer service and brand awareness.

We invite you to schedule a strategy session around the 5 steps Bryan has laid out in this chapter: https://1x1.xitx.com.

Economic Impacts of a Cyber Attack

By Leonard Galati

Drawing from a saying that a stitch in time saves nine, I share with you the story of a company that met its cyber-attack waterloo due to negligence. The engineering firm, located in New York City, was hit by a ransomware attack when an employee innocently opened an email that infected all of the critical files on the firm's servers. Within a few hours of this unfortunate occurrence, all 90 employees were stopped in their tracks from a production standpoint. Operations came to a screeching halt, and so did pending and incoming revenue. As if these were not enough, the cyber attack also rendered all of the firm's design files, which equated to twenty years of hard work, useless.

It is a well-known fact that the economic and psychological impacts of a cyber attack can be devastating. This cyber attack had an immediate adverse effect on the firm's current multi-million dollar projects. Not only did the firm's building construction projects stop, connections with potential clients were also lost. For every day of the period while the attack lasted, the firm lost $50,000. These, altogether, led to irreparable damage to the reputation of the firm, which would hamper its ability to win future contracts. While it is normal to sympathize with this firm over this untold hardship, you are definitely going to blame its management after knowing some of the firm's sensitive decisions regarding the protection of its data before the cyber attack.

A team of information technology (IT) experts had earlier approached the firm to help improve its cybersecurity for a moderate fee, but the firm's management turned down the offer for different reasons, including cost of the deal. But if the firm had had an idea of what was imminent, it wouldn't hesitate to pay twice the fee proposed by the IT team to help tighten its cybersecurity. Apart from the loss of revenue, client confidence levels were dropping rapidly. Current contracts were in jeopardy of being breeched, and the firm's ability to deliver was at a standstill. Eventually, it was the same IT team whose offer was turned down that led the firm in the journey of recovering the data, although it did not come on a silver platter.

The tech team went into disaster recovery mode and checked the local backups, only to discover that the hackers had deleted them. With 10 terabytes of data involved; restoration would take weeks from the offsite cloud backup. Hence, the firm decided to pay the ransom of $10,000 demanded by the hackers to unlock the files, as that was the quickest option available for the firm to get back on its feet and become operational again. As part of the process to pay the ransom, a bitcoin account had to be established. Thus, a Google search was made to hire a bitcoin broker quickly to fast track the transaction. After exchanging emails and texts, the exchange was made, and the firm waited for the bitcoin funds to hit its digital wallet, but it never did. The bitcoin broker duped them for $10,000. This just added insult to injury.

With very few choices, they were forced to find another bitcoin broker. This time they were a bit more selective. By this time, it was 3 a.m. on a Saturday, and all parties involved were, to say the least, restless. Luckily, this time, the funds hit, and the ransom was paid. The unlock key was received, and the IT team rushed to a computer to free the files. The team followed the instructions to enter the key and launch the decryptor. As they waited with bated breath, nothing was happening. The decryptor would crash upon each launch. It wasn't working, and the files weren't unlocking. The owner of the firm erupted into a volcano of rage, spewing expletives into the air. Having just lost $20,000, he sweeps his arm across his desk, clearing it of all objects.

Resorting to cloud backup restore, it took two weeks to get the data back. The cyberattack resulted in a $500,000 loss in revenue, clients seeking retribution for their losses, and an undeterminable amount of damage to their reputation. The owners decided to revisit the cybersecurity proposal presented six months earlier and implement the recommendations to improve their security posture. You could see the pen slightly bow as the owner signed the agreement venting his frustration through the ballpoint, nearly tearing the paper.

In this chapter, we'll discuss what a cyber attack is, why a cyber attack is a problem/threat, its effects on businesses, and why now is the ideal time to protect your data from an attack.

What Is a Cyber Attack and Why Is It a Problem?

In simple terms, a cyber attack is an assault launched by cybercriminals using one or more computers against a single or multiple computers or networks. There are many ways hackers achieve this. One popular method is through the use of botnets. Botnets comprise a network of computers that have been compromised and placed under the mothership's control. The mothership is operated by the cybercriminal, who in turn manipulates the child botnets. Next, the criminal will issue commands to the computers to carry out their attacks. Commands could be to have your computers send out emails, infect other devices, or perform a slew of other nefarious activities. Once this happens, you've lost control of your computers and probably won't even realize it.

Stealing from bank accounts is another common use for botnets. Malware on infected machines will wait for the victims to connect to their bank account. Then wait and allow the victim to authenticate. Subsequently, the bot will take over the connection and inject its own bank transfer commands into the system. To cover his tracks, the criminal will hide those transactions from the victims when they look at their balance. You can't trust what you see on the screen; it's what they want you to see.

Another method of delivery is through malicious email. It is estimated the one in every 300 emails contains malware. However, even if you are really careful opening email, there are other vulnerabilities, akin to a game of whack-a-mole. Another attack method is hacking social media accounts. Criminals will hack social networking accounts and seed malicious links to bad URLs, infecting those who click and visit that site. This is called a drive-by install. It enables hackers to harvest your account details and divert your money to their own untraceable digital wallets.

Lastly, cybercriminals also make use of denial-of-service (DDoS) attacks. Similar to a mafia protection racket, DDoS attacks are used to disrupt the transactions of target companies, usually those with a high level of online activity. Cybercriminals will threaten to prevent a company from using its website for its purposes or even take it down for some time unless they are paid. If the company refuses to pay them, then criminals send a command to their botnets to start flooding the company website with requests. Typical payments are between $10,000 and $50,000. These mean that cyber attacks pose a great threat to the safety of companies' money, privacy, and data. A cyber attack is, therefore, a common enemy to all companies, and it is a problem that must be prevented.

Economic Effects of Cyber Attacks on Businesses

With faster internet speeds and more businesses leveraging the internet for operations, cyber attacks directly affect every business in one way or the other. As the employee size of companies increase, the threat of a cyber-security breach grows, and the damage that it will cause is exponential. Today, all companies rely on technology. Due to this, companies need to make cybersecurity a top priority, but most don't. Many organizations operate on outdated network infrastructures, vulnerable software, and have a fundamental lack of security. Since the task of protecting our networks from hackers is one of the significant challenges that we will face over the next few decades, if not longer, a cyber attack stands to be one of the biggest problems of any business in the world. When a company falls victim to an adverse cyber event, it may face a range of loss, ranging from those that are easy to observe and quantify to those that are not. Listed below are some real possibilities.

- Loss of IP
- Loss of strategic Information
- Increased cost of capital
- Reputational damage
- Loss of data and equipment
- Loss of revenue
- Cybersecurity improvements
- Bad PR
- Customer protection
- Regulatory penalties
- Court settlements and fees
- Breach notifications
- Forensics

The effect of adverse cyber events on small and medium-sized businesses usually leads to premature fold up. IP theft could wipe out the firm's entire livelihood. Similarly, a business disruption that lasts several days could cause customers to abandon a small firm permanently. Finally, the fixed costs of dealing with a breach or attack, such as the cost of cybersecurity improvements and legal fees, would represent a larger fraction of a small firm's operating budget. In the light of this, every business has to take necessary preventive measures to avoid being attacked. No business is free from the possible scourge of cyber attacks as hackers target any industry they can profit from.

The 2015 Year-End Economic Report of the National Small Business Association (2015) estimated that, based on survey evidence from 884 small-business owners, 42 percent of respondents experienced exposure breach or an attack.[1] Also, small and medium-sized businesses are at a high risk of being attacked by ransomware, which renders a firm's files inaccessible until a ransom is paid. They are also prone to attacks that exploit weaknesses in email systems in order to trick firms into transferring large sums of money into the perpetrators' bank accounts. According to the survey, an adverse cyber event costs the victim company over $7,000 on average. For small businesses whose business banking accounts were hacked, the average loss was $32,000. For the median company in the same study, in terms of revenues, these numbers represent, respectively, 0.28 percent and 1.28 percent of firm revenue. Although these are fairly low numbers, events are typically underreported, and the firms in the survey likely only quantify immediate and easily observable losses.

---

[1]https://www.nsba.biz/wp-content/uploads/2016/02/Year-End-Economic-Report-2015.pdf

Countermeasures

Did you know that cybercrime is a 1.5 trillion-dollar industry? Yes, I just referred to it as an industry – that is sad but true. Cybercrime is a big business, and the business is good for hackers. Hackers invest a lot of time and effort into different activities that help them map out efficient strategies of hijacking your data due to this reason. The implication of this, thus, is that you equally have to strive to protect your data from cyber attacks if you do not want to bear the consequences discussed above. Different protective measures that can help you keep your files safe against all forms of cyber attack are discussed below.

Defense in depth is a concept used in information security in which multiple layers of security controls (defense) are placed throughout an IT system. Its intent is to provide redundancy in the event a security control fails or a vulnerability is exploited so as to cover aspects of personnel, procedural, technical, and physical security for the duration of the system's life cycle. Being a layering tactic, the idea behind the defense-in-depth approach is to defend a system against any particular attack, using several independent methods. Defense in depth can be divided into three areas: Physical, Technical, and Administrative.

1. Physical Controls: anything that physically limits or prevents access to IT systems.

Fences, guards, dogs, CCTV systems, and the like belong to this category.

2. Technical Controls: hardware or software, the purpose of which is to protect systems and resources. Examples of technical controls are disk encryption, fingerprint readers, and authentication. Hardware technical controls differ from physical controls in that they prevent access to the contents of a system, but not the physical systems themselves.

3. Administrative Controls: an organization's policies and procedures. Their purpose is to ensure that there is proper guidance available in regard to security, and that regulations are met. They include things such as hiring practices, data handling procedures, and security requirements.

Furthermore, the onus of cybersecurity responsibility falls on the shoulders of an organization's management who have to ensure that the proper safeguards are in place. This is a daunting task, especially when attacks are coming from every direction, but it is a responsibility one must bear. Vulnerabilities include mobile devices, PCs, servers, cloud applications, email, websites, control systems (IoT), and, last but not least, humans. Unfortunately, there's no magic bullet. Defense in depth is the best strategy, and it is achieved through a layered approach. A multitude of tools must be utilized to mitigate threats from multiple attack vectors. I've put together a list of safeguards that should be on your radar.

1. Security Assessment: It's important to establish a baseline and close existing vulnerabilities. When was your last assessment? Get a certified cybersecurity professional to do this on a routine basis.

2. Email Security: Secure your email with enhanced security features like email filtering, block email fraud, URL validation, and attachment scanning. Basic antispam is not enough.

3. Password Security: Apply security policies on your network. Examples: Deny or limit USB file storage access, enable enhanced password policies, set user screen timeouts, and limit user access.

4. Security Awareness Training: Utilize services to train your users – often! Teach them about data security, email attacks, and your policies and procedures. The human firewall is one of your biggest weak spots.

5. Advanced Endpoint Security: Protect your computers and data from malware, viruses, and cyber-attacks with advanced endpoint security. Regular antivirus won't cut it anymore. Today's latest technology can even rollback a ransomware attack.

6. Dark Web Research: Utilize a dark web scanning service. Knowing in real-time what

passwords and accounts have been exposed on the dark web will allow you to be proactive in preventing a data breach.

7. Security Incident & Event Management (SIEM): Use a SIEM product to collect logs from machines and network devices, review data, correlate data with threat intelligence feeds, and deliver actionable intelligence to thwart attacks.

8. Web Security: Internet security is a race against time. Use web security products to detect threats as they emerge on the internet and block them within seconds – before they reach the user.

9. Encryption: Enable hard drive encryption and encrypted file systems whenever possible. The goal is to encrypt files at rest, in motion (think file transfer), and especially on laptops.

10. Backup & Disaster Recovery: Backup local and offsite to the cloud. Include in your DR plan a way to spin up servers and access data in the event of a disaster. Test backups periodically.

In summary, the impact of a cyber attack on a business can be very devastating. Revenue would not be the only concern. There's reputation, investments, and the effects on your clients. At this point it's apparent that being attached to the internet can be very dangerous and the best approach is to strengthen your security posture.

Taking the defense-in-depth mindset with a layered approach to security will afford a company the best chance at staying out of harm's way.

About the Author

Over the last 30 years, Leonard Galati has gone from defending our nation as a U.S. Marine to protecting global businesses as the CEO of CyberTeam, a private IT and cybersecurity firm. His zeal for network security led him into the world of information technology after nine years of active service as a Marine. In order to help as many organizations as possible to protect their data from cyber attacks, he launched CyberTeam in 1998, serving the tristate New York area. As a Certified Information Systems Security Professional (CISSP), he has been running cybersecurity programs for his clients with unwavering dedication to his craft.

Leonard Galati conforms to best practices, and the NIST framework has been his standard. Through his vCIO consultations and programs, clients have benefited greatly and, as result, steer clear of cyber attacks. His wealth of experience as the CEO of CyberTeam translated into a chapter of this book. It is, therefore, accurate to say that Leonard Galati contributed to this book to communicate with a larger audience from all walks of life regarding the dangers of cyber attacks and recommendation to help mitigate risk solutions posed by the inherent dangerous nature of the internet.

Storm Clouds Are Forming

By Roy Leffew

"I need your help!" said the voice at the other end of the phone. I could hear the undercurrent of panic in his voice. His business was in jeopardy. He needed some advice and real solutions if he was going to weather the current economic storm raging against his business.

His call may have been the first, but I would have at least a dozen more that week, all with a similar tone. An economic storm front was moving in and stalling over the entire country – over the entire world. Businesses would have to pivot overnight in order to survive. Suddenly the world was changing, and the modus operandi of yesterday would no longer work. Technology would take a leading role in ensuring the pivot would be successful, or the lack thereof would result in the untimely death of a dream.

The details of this particular "storm" are beside the point. Storms come. Storms pass. Businesses with a foundation built to withstand such storms survive.

Businesses that fail to develop that foundation fail. The playing field is never level. There are no guarantees. There is no "sure thing." There is no success without planning, struggling, evaluating, and planning again. Storms come...but the prudent prepare. Storms come...but the wise understand. Storms come...but the nimble pivot quickly. You know all of that. You are here, reading this, because you are different. You are intimately aware of the fragility involved in running a business, and you are looking for an insurance policy to protect you when the next storm threatens. Congratulations! Take a seat, lean back, absorb and act on the advice in this book and you will be ready when the storms come. Let the winds blow, the seas rage, the lightning strike – you will be ready.

Jim Collins, in his book Good to Great, advises that the best way to use technology is as "an accelerator of momentum rather than a creator of it." Though his book was originally published in 2001, six years before the first iPhone was released, Collins' advice is even more valid today. Technology advances quickly, but it is only a tool that, when managed correctly, can accelerate a business during times of crisis. Likewise, if not managed, not well thought out, and not implemented with a strategic eye, it will also accelerate the decline of a business. It is easy to make the mistake of getting caught up in the latest technology and looking at it to solve all problems. So rather than espouse the latest technology in this chapter, we will instead look at the "concepts" of technology that you need to have in place to weather upcoming storms. We will walk through the technology foundation that can keep you nimble, help you manage your workforce, and lead to increased productivity. This foundation will be your protective umbrella to help you weather the coming storms.

Marketing Storm

One of the most important things you can do to be prepared for a "pivot" in the midst of a changing environment is to have a fully functional marketing "system" in place. This is accomplished using a series of marketing funnels. There are entire books dedicated to setting up marketing funnels, but for the scope of this chapter, you should be aware of what a "funnel" is and that there are software products which help you automate these funnels. A marketing funnel provides potential customers with the right messaging at the right time to speak to their interests. The idea is to attract potential customers through messaging, track who they are (basic demographics), what they need (problems you can solve), and provide incentives (free valuable information) to motivate them to establish and maintain a relationship with you. The messaging can be in countless forms from digital to print but all contain a "call to action" on the part of the interested party. Once the "call to action" has been executed, you now have valuable data that needs to be tracked and utilized.

First, the "call to action" should be specific to the messaging so you know what problem to address for them. You know about their need or pain point for which you have solutions. The "call to action," while giving away something valuable, asks the participant for something valuable: full contact information or a simple email address. Receiving this, you have a direct line of communication to the prospective customer and know something about a problem they are trying to solve. You'll be able to use automation to route them through your process based on their preferences and behaviors while maintaining a personal touch. Employing the following marketing automation tools, you'll manage this relationship throughout its various stages.

- Customer Relationship Management (CRM) – a software application that helps you keep track of your company's relationships and communications with customers and potential customers. Discover a lead, manage the lead through various levels of interest, move the lead into a qualified prospect, and then develop a customer relationship by providing a timely solution. CRM solutions track follow-up efforts, schedule subsequent actions, and produce predictable results.

- Drip Campaigns and Lead Nurturing – a software application where a predefined series of actions happen for a given prospect or customer. A drip campaign can be set up with the goal of increasing your brand's awareness, helping turn a prospect into a customer, or simply engaging and retaining current customers. The actions in a campaign might be to automate sending various emails at specific intervals. It may include follow-up phone calls and/or appointments as certain thresholds are met. New campaigns can be designed and executed any time you need to pivot your messaging during a "storm," allowing you to bring along your valuable contacts as your business model grows and changes. Imagine being able to communicate directly to anyone who has ever expressed interest in your company at the push of a button with whatever message you have at that moment. You have just imagined the power of automated marketing.

Analytics Storm

Another key in surviving a storm is having accurate data to lead you through decision processes. It is not enough just to know how to read a Profit & Loss Statement (P&L). You need much more granular information to make quick decisions to navigate during a storm. You cannot wait until the monthly or quarterly reports is posted, you need yesterday's, or in some cases, the last hour's numbers. You want to plan for and implement an accounting application that can provide you with the numbers you need, when you need them. How are sales affected? Which customers are purchasing which products? Has the cost of goods increased? What are the new margins?

The information needed for these analytics are most commonly found in a billing/point of sale system, a purchasing application, a stock/inventory system, a job costing application, and a payroll system, among others. Wouldn't it be preferable to combine these applications into a single integrated accounting system? Otherwise, you'll spend too much time and money trying to get data from one system, then merge it with data from another system in order to have accurate information to provide critical answers.

Dispersed Workforce Storm

Often in a storm, you'll find yourself separated from those you need the most. Whether by choice or by force, remote workers will be a reality. You need a plan for how disparate employees in diverse locations can collaborate so that productivity does not suffer. Search for and implement a collaborative software application that provides the following:

- **Central management of documents and files** – The first solution for a dispersed workforce is to provide for structured data access. If your data exists solely on an office server somewhere, you'll have challenges giving staff access to data with the ease they need to be productive. You need to provide a secure mechanism by which the right people can access the right data when they need it. A well-considered data structure that separates documents and data based on functionality and users who need access to the data is essential. The application should permit access of the data based on the role of an individual, allowing for the level of access to change person by person. Some will need "read-only" access; others will need the ability to create, modify, and delete data files. The application should track who accessed what data file and when. It should be able easily to restore previous versions of the file in the event of accidental deletion or modification. The data should be able to be accessed by whatever device the individual is using at any given time, so weigh mobile device access availability highly.

- **Collaboration Tools** – The application you choose must provide a structure for various employees and in some cases vendors, to access the information needed for a given project or customer. Data regarding a project is often scattered about in different files, email communications, phone calls, messages, etc. Look for an application that allows you to combine all these data points into a central area to record every aspect of the project or customer. A real-time communication platform is vital to allow team members to communicate quickly with each other via chat, messaging, and voice/video calls. Members will need to work on the same document or piece of information at the same time, so a preferable application would allow multiple people to access and edit a document at the same time.

- **External Data Sharing** – This application should provide for sharing of files with external entities. Ideally, you will be able to control whether an outside entity has the ability to modify the data, add files, or simply be able to read data posted for them. Avoid using email as a distribution system of external files where you have no control of the data once it has left your possession. Instead, the external data sharing application should provide features to allow you to share data, provide constructs of access, allow logging and notification of access, and, most importantly, provide the ability to revoke access and remotely wipe data on demand. In this way, control of your data lies solely with you and your staff.

- **Security** – While overall security concerns for a dispersed workforce are addressed in other chapters, the important thing to consider for your collaborative software application is to provide rich security features for accessing the data contained therein. Individualized login credentials, including two-factor authentication, are highly recommended. Data should be encrypted when at rest. The application should provide for an individual belonging to multiple groups or teams, each with its own set of security and access rules. Secure logging of who accessed which data at what time is also essential for maintaining security and reporting.

Customer Engagement Storm

Most businesses engage their customers in a way that makes the most sense to them or is easiest for them. Unfortunately, during a storm, continued engagement by the customer cannot be guaranteed to continue in a specific manner. Thought must be given to all the methods a customer may prefer to employ to engage your business. Thinking through these variations and providing a pathway into your sales cycle for them will keep you nimble in a storm. Look for applications that can deliver unified communication for you and your customers that includes access through voice, text, email, chat, website, and various social media channels. Customers may prefer to engage physically, or they may wish to be impersonal. Giving them the option to choose will allow you to reach the broadest spectrum of customers as they are ready to buy.

Next, think about how you deliver your solution. Think through the question, "If I were unable to deliver my solution this way, how else might I provide the solution?" Again, what makes the most sense to you might not be the way the customer would like to engage the delivery of your solution. Seek ways to offer multiple delivery mechanisms based on the choice of the customer. Revisiting the CRM application mentioned earlier, use this application to store and retrieve customer preferences for a tailored approach to each customer. A couple of years ago, we might not have imagined that someone would want or require fast food or groceries to be delivered to their home – nor did we envision it would be possible. We certainly never thought a doctor's appointment could take place over the internet. Today, these situations are commonplace.

Finally, implement a structured follow-up and quality control feature with your customers. Maintaining consistent customer feedback regarding what you did right or wrong helps you keep your finger on the pulse of success for your business. CRM applications should incorporate the ability to solicit feedback from your customer at each point of contact. Use it and analyze the results often to make course corrections quickly.

The weather may be clear today, the forecast may be sunny skies and warm nights, but don't be fooled into a false sense of security. A storm is brewing. The time for preparation for the storm has come. You've been given the basic outline for the items needed for your storm shelter:

- Marketing Automation Solutions
- Real-Time Analytic Solutions
- Remote Workforce Solutions
- Customer Engagement Solutions

Remember, failing to plan for the storm is a plan for failing during the storm. Take the time needed today to research, trial, and implement the solutions that will make you impervious to the coming storm's mighty blow. I hear thunder in the distance, do you?

About the Author

Roy Leffew is CEO and owner of Grace Computer Resources, Inc., an IT services and cyber security business in the Metro Atlanta, Georgia, area, which has been in business for 35 years. An entrepreneur at heart, Roy has a passion for seeing business owners succeed against overwhelming odds. He specializes in making technology and security understandable, managing a company's day-to-day IT, helping to implement productivity tools, and guiding a business owner through strategic technology planning. His heart is captured by Terri, his wife of 36 years, his confidante and head cheerleader. He is the father of four (and their spouses) but is perhaps most excited about being "Papa" to his five grandchildren.

Schedule a free consultation with Roy Leffew at https://GraceComputer.com/freeconsult

How to Ensure Employees' Computers Are Secure While Working at Home

By Jason Penka

I've spent over 20 years in the technology information industry. During that time, I have seen a shift in how businesses manage their employees. At the turn of the century, your business data was stored and protected on massive servers and housed in your office. Companies built dedicated server rooms and controlled access to the data from within the company network. As the internet evolved, that data become more distributed, as so did the workforce. Businesses started to allow employees to access that data from home, while on vacation, or working from a remote office. Information now resides in the cloud and can be accessed by anyone, anywhere, and at any time. This includes cyber criminals and they have now found a new easy method to access your company data.

My current company, Tech Junkies, has been working with clients for the past 13 years. We started our business helping consumers fix and secure their home computers. Quickly we added support for businesses. However, unlike many other IT companies that started with consumer support, we never abandoned our residential client base. In fact, we did the exact opposite. We developed a core function of our business to FOCUS on residential users. We wanted to bring enterprise-level technology to consumers, home-based business, and small-office clients. Currently, we support thousands of residential and small businesses across the United States.

So why didn't we do as most IT companies, and drop the residential support? Why not focus 100% on business clients? That decision came after working with a small-business owner several years ago. Jane (not her real name) has a successful financial services business with about 25 employees. Jane's business was providing financial planning services to her clients. She handled everything from insurance to retirement account management. When her clients retired, she transitioned to help them manage their retirement assets to ensure their nest egg never ran out. Her business was booming.

I met Jane when she was just a start up. She was working from her house and had a handful of clients. We did support for her personal computer that she was also using for business. As her business grew, so did our offerings for business level support. When Jane signed a lease on a new office to move her growing staff into, we did a full hardware refresh and replaced all of the workstations with new desktops, three monitors, and brand new servers to house the company data. Jane's business was growing faster than her technology budget could keep up. Landing a new client was an expensive process and it took time to recoup those costs through management fees.

Slowly over time, Jane started to handle more and more of her IT in-house. This was usually handled by the current office manager, who was usually replaced for one reason or another about every other year. We continued to keep in touch, but she just couldn't justify the expense for us to manage her IT. One day, Jane calls, "Good news," she said. "I'm looking to upgrade all of my computers and server. I need your help!" I sat down with Jane, her office manager, and newly hired CFO. We performed a full technology assessment and presented an action plan to Jane and her team. Jane's company data consisted mostly of sensitive financial, medical, and personal information for her clients. These files were either scans of originals or simply Word or Excel files. The software and applications she used had all moved to a cloud-based model. Within our action plan, we presented Jane with new workstations, but replaced the server with a secure file hosting and sharing application. As with all of our action plans, we always offer two options: 1) You can take this plan and implement it yourself or 2) you can have us do it for you.

Jane's new CFO decided he could do the implementation himself, with some help from the office manager, and save a lot of money. Jane decided to have us perform a project to replace the workstations. She had us then wipe and reload the old computers so her staff could take them home. She thought it would be a nice gesture to give them a free computer. We performed the replacement and prepared the old computers for her employees to use at home. At the time, we were at a crossroads with our company. We had been getting pressure from our consultants and advisors to abandon our residential service plans. We halfheartedly offered our CloudCare Secure program to Jane's employees as a discounted rate. They all declined.

What happened three months later sticks with me today. I get a call from Jane. I could tell from her voice on the phone that she was shaken. Tearfully, she asked me to come to her office right away. I headed down to Jane's office and when I walked in and it was like walking in on a funeral. I sat down with Jane, her office manager, and the CFO. The CFO starts to tell me the story of what has happened since I was last there three months ago.

The CFO, looking to complete this project under budget, was looking for cheaper alternatives to all of the technology advice we had offered. He decided the cheapest file sharing software that worked for the company was DropBox. They purchased a consumer account and just shared access among 20 different employees. The CFO continued to cut corners. He purchased a consumer-grade firewall from Sam's Club. He re-installed the older Microsoft Office version (even thought it was close to end-of-life support). He skipped the anti-virus software and just utilized Windows Defender since it was pre-installed on the computers and free.

With their core applications all moved to the cloud, the staff started to figure out they could just install DropBox on their home computers and access all the company files there. Jane loved this because they could help their clients all hours of the day and all days of the week. When employees were sick, they just worked from home. This would reduce costs and increase productivity. About one month in, they started to see strange problems. New computers were running slow, files went missing then reappeared, and computers would randomly crash for no reason.

I was then informed that two weeks ago a message popped up on all their computers. It stated that their company data has been encrypted. They had to pay a ransom of $200 to get it back. This was on every computer that had DropBox installed. It affected the company data and the home computers of the employees. Some employees had seen it spread to other personal computers through a personal DropBox account they used to store family photos and personal financial information. So not only did the company just lose all of its data, but its employees just lost all of their family photos, videos, music, and documents as well. The CFO jumped into action and quickly figured out how to pay the ransom.

After two days the hackers contacted them to de-crypt the data. That was when the real problem started. The hackers recognized that Jane's company was in the financial services sector. They also realized they didn't infect 1 or 2 computers but 40 computers. The ransom instantly went from $200 to $250,000. They were able to negotiate that amount down to $25,000. The CFO arranged for payment through Bitcoin. Then silence. They heard nothing from the hackers. That was when the reality of the situation really set in. This would bankrupt Jane. She lost all of her company data and was out $25,000. Her employees were devastated as well. They had lost all their personal information. Family photos of vacations, concerts, days at the lake ... gone.

Luckily for Jane, we have a policy to take a full backup of any computer on which we work. We normally purge the backups after 30 days. However, this project was large enough that we stored the backups on dedicated storage devices. We had the data from her old server, too. We even kept the backups from the employee's computers. They had only lost 3 months of data. It took us 3 full weeks to get Jane back up and running. However, the investigation told the real story of how this happened.

As part of her insurance claim, we had to investigate how the breach occurred. We worked with a security solutions provider to track the entry point of the virus. We discovered it originated from a personal email account of one of her employees. He clicked on a list for an advertisement that looked like a credit card offer from Cabella's (a sporting goods store in the area). The virus installed on his personal computer. Since the company used DropBox and had it installed across company and personal computers, the virus spread without any problem. Some employees were using their new computer from Jane for personal use as well. They stored home photos, personal files, and even let their kids use the computer. This employee had a personal DropBox account. It was installed on three of his personal computers and, as we found out, the computer he used for work, the computer he got from Jane.

All told, Jane was able to get back up and running. For about 6 months. Her insurance didn't cover the claim against the cyber attack because she didn't take the necessary precautions to protect her network. During the investigation, we found that the hackers had moved the original version of the files to their own servers. This meant the data would be on the dark web at some point. Jane was then responsible for telling all her clients about the breach. She was required by law to pay a fine and provide credit monitoring for each account that was compromised. The total cost of just the credit monitoring totaled over half a million dollars. Jane had to file for bankruptcy protection. Her existing clients were sold to a competitor and she went to work for her.

After seeing what Jane had gone through, I had to think to myself, maybe I should have worked harder to at least keep the home computers protected. We could have discovered what was going on early and stopped it before it spread to the company. With more people working from home, their vacation house, restaurants, coffee shops... really anywhere, they need the same protection that larger companies need. But it has to scale to their level and make sense for them. That was when we got to work on developing a plan for companies to ensure employees' at home computers are kept protected.

Oddly enough, we handle the IT for the company for which Jane is currently working. One thing that came over from Jane's company was the work-from-home culture. Many of Jane's employees went to work for the same company. They expressed a desire to continue to work from home when needed. As more and more of our technology moves into the cloud, this conversation is going to continue to come up across businesses of all sizes. From corporate America to small businesses on Main Street, this can be a double-edged sword.

As more employees look for more flexibility in their work lives, business owners are feeling the pressure to put in place some level of technology to allow them to work from home. At the time of the writing this book (June 2020), we are going through the COVID-19 pandemic. We have seen a substantial increase in work from home due to state and nationwide stay-at-home orders. However, I want to present some statistics that were pulled before COVID-19 brought this work from home movement to light.

A special analysis dene by FlexJobs and Global Workplace Analytics found that there has been an upward trend in the number of people working remotely.[2] From 2016 to 2017, work from home grew 7.9%. Over the last five years, it grew 44% and over the previous 10 years it grew 91%. Between 2005 and 2017, there was a 159% increase in work from home. The same study finds that 90% of employees say more flexible arrangements would increase morale.[3]

Working from home can help attract and retain talent. Of those surveyed, 80% say they would turn down a job that didn't offer flexible working.[4] It's so important to them that 33% say they would

---

[2]https://www.flexjobs.com/blog/post/remote-work-statistics/#:~:text=Remote%20Work%20Is%20Increasing&text=Over%20the%20last%20five%20years,or%203.4%25%20of%20the%20population.

[3] https://www.flexjobs.com/blog/post/flexjobs-gwa-report-remote-growth/

[4] https://www.crainsnewyork.com/sponsored-future-work/work-life-integration-customized-approach

prioritize such an arrangement over having a more prestigious role. In Crain's Future of Work survey, more than three-fourths of respondents cited flexible schedules and remote work as the most effective non-monetary ways to retain employees.

So why do many businesses see this as a problem? The cost in building a work from home program can seem overwhelming. Your business already has a computer you provide for your employees. Do they take them home? Do you buy them a new computer? Do you replace the desktops with laptops? Should the employees just use their own personal computers? If you look at the costs of allowing a 50-person company to transition to allow flexible schedules with a work-from-home program, the hardware costs alone can reach to $100,000. This is why many businesses have been allowing employees to just use their personal computers.

The problem with this approach is it's basically like having a screen door on a submarine. When employees can access your company data from their personal, non-secure, non-managed computer, you're inviting cyber criminals to feast on your company data. During the start of the COVID-19 pandemic, thousands of businesses had to find a way to transition their workforce to a work-from-home model almost overnight. Concessions were made that opened massive vulnerabilities in their company's network security. Initially, this was thought to be a temporary solution. As time went on, the lockdown was extended. Employees were settling in at home and staying productive. However, most companies didn't address the cyber security concerns until after the lockdowns. As I write this book, data breaches are reaching an all-time high.[5] Cyber criminals are having a field day with the work-from-home movement.

How, then, do you correctly implement working from home and keep your employees' computers protected and your company data safe? First, you need to start with a plan. I've outlined below three separate viewpoints on building a strategy that will keep everyone involved protected. We move the focus away from "Work from Home" to a "Work from Anywhere" strategy. You want your plan to be able to grow and breathe with your business.

Work from Anywhere Strategy # 1: Employees Use Their Personal Computers

Implementing a full Work-from-Anywhere prog-ram overnight can be overwhelming; starting by letting a few key employees work from home using their own computers is a great way to test the waters. In these cases, you want to limit the direct access to company data from the employees' home computer. This strategy works well when your employee is working from home between 10% and 25% of the time.

---

[5] https://digitalguardian.com/blog/history-data-breaches

1. Provide Remote Access to Their Work Computer. This can be accomplished with remote access third-party software, such as ScreenConnect, Splashtop, or LogMeIn. All three of these solutions provide business-level security and can be set up and deployed by your IT provider or in-house IT department. This secure connection will ensure your company data does not leave your internal network. For companies just getting started with Work from Anywhere, we deploy Splashtop. This is an easy-to-use software with a low cost of deployment.

2. Provide a Security Suite for Employees' Computer. Have your IT provider install business grade anti-virus, web filtering, and patch management software on the employees' computer. This will ensure a stable and secure platform to access their work computer. If your current IT provider or internal IT department does not wish to support a home computer, then look for an outside provider to help with this portion of the support. We have a division of our company that handles residential clients. We utilize the same enterprise-level technology but have a separate tier for the support and service desk.

3. Establish a Secure Virtual Private Network (VPN) Connection. A VPN connection can be provided using most enterprise-grade

firewalls. This will allow you to create a secure method for your employee to connect to the company network using only a software application. This keeps internet traffic behind your company firewall while connected to its office computer.

Work from Anywhere Strategy # 2: Company-Owned Equipment

By far the best option when creating a Work-from-Anywhere program is to have the company own all the hardware being used by the employee. While this does increase the up-front costs, it allows you a measured level of control and security for your business. This is another option that can be implemented over time. This option works well when your employee is working from home between 25% and 50% of the time.

1. **Replicate Their Office Workstation.** Provide the employees with the same configuration they have at the office. This could include multiple monitors if that is what their office workstation includes. We even recommend purchasing a printer if it's necessary for their job. In most cases their productivity software can be licensed on this computer without an additional cost. We utilize Microsoft Office 365, which allows for each user to install the software on up to 5 devices.

2. **Provide a Business-Level Firewall.** This step is great if most of their remote work is

performed in the same location, such as a home office. The employee will get the added benefit of advanced security, performance, and stability while you add an additional level of security for your business. This allows you to establish a hardware VPN back to your office that is always on. We recommend the Ubiquiti Dream Machine for a budget option and the Sophos XG 106 for a more secure option. Both firewalls can be set up with multiple local networks, allowing the employee to separate his/her personal computers from your business computer.

3. **Install Remote Management and Monitoring Software.** Your IT provider should consider this computer as an extension of your internal network. It should get the same protections and support as any other computer. Ensure software is installed for anti-virus, web filtering, patch management, and cyber protection. We install the same agents and software on at-home computers as we do for the internal network. Employees call the same support desk number and we treat and support that computer like any other on the network.

4. **Encrypt the Computer.** Install encryption software on the computer. This will ensure that none of the data stored on the computer can be access in the event the computer is stolen.

Work from Anywhere Strategy # 3: Transition to a Fully Mobile Workforce

As you grow your company and you see more of your staff requiring a work-from-home option, it starts to make sense to take your Work from Anywhere strategy to the next level. Using a lot of the same principles in the other two strategies, a fully mobile workforce allows your employees truly to work from anywhere in the world. Moving to this strategy effectively eliminates the possibility of a disaster shutting down your business. Along with the same recommendations in Strategy #2, we recommend you own all of the hardware, provide a business-level firewall, install remote management software, and encrypt the computer. In addition, we recommend the following:

1. **Provide a Mobile Workstation.** We recommend you find a portable laptop such as a Dell Latitude 7000 series, Microsoft Surface, or MacBook that can act as the primary computer for your employee. Still include external monitors for an at-home desk configuration with additional screen real estate. This allows you to look at smaller laptops such as a 14" or 13". The smaller laptop size allows more flexibility and freedom when working outside of the house. If your employee is going to travel (for work or recreation) he/she can take the computer office along.

2. **Utilize a Unified Communications as a Service Platform.** With your employees working remotely, I recommend moving your phone system to a cloud-hosted platform like Cytracom. Not only can they have their business phone at their desk at home, but they can access their company phone through a desktop browser or their iPhone.

3. **Provide a Cell Phone.** Even through every employee has his/her personal cell phone, don't have him/her rely on that for business purposes. Give the employee a company cell phone with a good data plan. Not only does this keep your business communication unified, but it can act as a backup internet connection if the primary connection goes down. The employee can also use the phone's hotspot in restaurants and coffee shops when traveling instead of relying on free hot spots.

Next Steps to Building a Good Foundation

Every business is different. If there is one thing I have learned in my two decades working with businesses in technology, it's that a solution that works for one business doesn't always work for another. Each business has its own workflow processes, line of business applications, and company culture. The reality is that allowing employees to work from home is good for your employees and good for your business. But what are the next steps to take? How do you start laying that foundation?

The answer to that question differs for each business I encounter. Since you have purchased this book, I'm going to provide you and your company with a Free Strategy Call. This can be used for anything but I would recommend we talk about your next steps in moving your business to a work-from-anywhere model and how to keep those computers secure while at the employee's home.

You can book your call here:
https://Strategycall.tjunkies.com

About the Author

Jason Penka is a technology entrepreneur and Founder of CEO of Tech Junkies and Residential MSP Group both headquartered in Hays, Kansas. Serving Western Kansas since 2007, Tech Junkies focuses on servicing residential and small to midsized businesses with general IT management and cyber-security solutions. Residential MSP Group is Jason's most recent business venture.

Jason grew in a family of entrepreneurs and small business owners with companies ranging from retail to professional services. Unlike most IT business owners, Jason wanted to ensure those small business owners weren't left out when it came to utilizing technology. This led Ja-son to create a program within Tech Junkies called CloudCare Secure™. This program provides home and small business clients with enterprise class technology and cyber-security solutions at an affordable price.

After creating a truly unique service delivery model for technology and cyber-security solutions to residential and small offices through Tech Junkies, Jason founded Residential MSP Group (rMSP). rMSP is focused on help-ing other IT companies expand their businesses utilizing the CloudCare Secure™ program.

During college at Fort Hays State University he found his passion for business through leadership and entrepreneurship classes and projects. As a final project in his degree program Jason developed a business plan for a web development company. This plan would end up being the source material for what would become Tech Junkies. The plan was so well developed it was used as a template for the class going forward.

Jason enjoys working with small and midsized businesses to develop a technology plan that will help keep their company secure, help them reduce wasted time, and implement innovative technology. He serves on several local boards and committees including the Informatics Advisory Council at his alma mater FHSU.

When not helping people and businesses with technology, he can be found on the golf course, cooking, or at-tending a rock concert.

Jason Penka can be reached as follows:

jason@thetechjunkies.net

www.linkedin.com/in/jasonpenka

www.thetechjunkies.net

785-621-2445

https://www.facebook.com/OfficialJasonPenka

5 Things You Need to Do to Keep Your Business Running Smoothly

By Ryan O'Hara

When things are going well, it is human nature to avoid thinking of the bad things that can come along and ruin our good times. This is just as true in business as it is in everyday life. When we don't plan for bad things to happen, we get caught unprepared and that can have disastrous consequences for our businesses.

I've had many discussions with clients and prospects about their ability to work from some place other than their office. Many just shrug it off and tell me it just isn't something they need. Their employees work from the office and that is just the way it is. What if something were to happen that made working from the office difficult or even impossible? In good times, this can be a difficult question for some to wrap their heads around.

When the COVID-19 pandemic hit, many business owners found themselves in this very scenario. Many had a plan and they shifted gears seamlessly. I had been in touch with my clients regularly over the weeks before the shelter-in-place order was given for our state. As the situation developed, we started putting plans in place and within 24 hours of the order being given, they were "business as usual," safe and secure, working in their homes. Some were slightly less prepared and while they were able to function, had some difficulties that could have been avoided had some of our earlier recommendations been implemented. One client had an older analog phone system in place that we recommended upgrading for over a year to a more flexible VOIP system. When the shelter in place order came down, we spent the better part of a week trying to get their carrier to forward one of their lines to the owner's cell phone. During that time, they were missing incoming phone calls and when the forwarding was finally in place, the owner was forced to handle all incoming calls himself since the provider was only able to forward the line to a single number. It was not long after that the client approved the project to move to the VOIP system we had previously recommended.

A global pandemic was something that most people never considered as a possible impact on their business. As horrible as it was, it did manage to demonstrate to many business owners the importance of being prepared for ANYTHING.

While my clients were able to move to a work-from-home situation relatively smoothly, many businesses were not as prepared. Throughout the next couple of weeks, we fielded calls from businesses that had no plan and were caught completely off guard. They were not only struggling to be productive, but they were cutting corners with regard to security, and unknowingly heading down a path of even further disaster.

If I had to pick one group of people who were most prepared for a major worldwide disaster, it was cybercriminals. They pounced on the opportunity to take advantage of businesses that were not prepared. We saw some significant spikes in the number of threats our security tools were blocking. We also gained a few new clients when they were hit with breaches and ransomware as a result of skipping and ignoring security while trying to find ways to work from home without having a plan beforehand.

Making sure your business is prepared for some unknown catastrophe can be difficult. It's not just about planning for more common things like fires or flooding. You need to have a plan that can be modified or adapted quickly to a scenario that you never even considered. Your plan needs to be capable of being implemented quickly with little to no notice. For this chapter, I've put together five steps to ensure your business can run smoothly in the face of disasters, big or small.

1. Plan Ahead and Document

I cannot emphasize the importance of this step enough. Have a plan. Do not wait until an emergency occurs and then try and scramble to figure out what to do. Even if your plan does not address the emergency exactly, it is still better than having no plan at all. A documented business continuity plan can save your business in a crisis. I cannot tell you how many times I've spoken to a prospective client and not only did they not have a documented business continuity plan, but they had no idea what it was or why they would ever need one.

A business continuity plan is a documented process that a company can follow to ensure operations can continue in the event of an issue or disaster. This is where you will document many of the steps discussed in this chapter and formulate a plan of action to keep your business running in the face of a disaster. In addition to documenting the steps you need to take for any disaster scenario, make sure you also assign a leader or champion who will be responsible for putting the plan into action.

Another plan that every business should have documented is a disaster recovery plan. While similar to the continuity plan, a disaster recovery plan focuses more on the IT aspect of business operations. A disaster recovery plan should include steps and processes for ensuring the safety and stability of critical systems and data. You'll want to document where things are, where they are backed up, and prioritize the things that are mission-critical for business operation. Once the disaster has been assessed, having all of this information in one place will be a great help in putting a plan into action to get things back up and running quickly and effectively.

If your employees are not used to working outside of the office, they may have difficulty adjusting. I recommend that every company has a documented remote worker policy on file. This policy should state what is expected of the employee and what rules they need to follow when working remotely. Having staff work remotely on occasion is a great way to have them trained and prepared should a situation arise that requires them to do so.

2. Communications

Your company is going to struggle if you have issues with communication. Your customers need to be able to reach you and your staff needs to be able to communicate with each other. If disaster strikes with little notice, communications can be problematic without a proper plan in place.

Most companies are not going to stay in business if their customers cannot reach them. If you have an old analog phone system that can't be easily modified to route calls to someplace other than your office, you could be in trouble. I recommend investing in a good voice over internet protocol

(VOIP) phone system. These can be configured to be as simple or as complex as your business warrants. They can also be easily modified to route calls to multiple numbers simultaneously using different methods. So, if the phone normally rings on multiple phones in your office, you can adjust the settings to have those same calls ring to those employees' mobile phones in a work from home situation. VOIP phone systems are highly configurable and flexible. With the right plan in place, you can quickly pivot from working in the office to working from home without it impacting your callers.

Now that your customers can reach you, what about internal communications? You can't just pop into a co-worker's office with a question if you are all working remotely. You probably don't want your staff on the phone all day and email can be problematic for quick conversations. Having a web or software-based collaboration tool can keep the flow of communication going for your employees while working remotely. Collaboration tools offer real-time text-based communication and many also offer the ability to switch quickly to a voice or video conversation as well. Groups or rooms can even be set up for specific projects where several people can communicate and collaborate on a topic.

What about in-person meetings? If the ability to meet with people in person is affected by the disaster and you are not able to meet face to face, there are an abundance of video conferencing tools available. I'm a firm believer that face-to-face conversations are more productive than interactions over the phone or email. I highly encourage you to take advantage of video conferencing tools in the event of a disaster when you cannot meet in person. This goes not only for owners, but staff as well. Some people might be shy or uncomfortable at first, but, in my experience, using video to communicate is considerably more productive and effective.

3. Work from Anywhere

Shifting from 100% of your staff working from the office to 100% of your staff working remotely is a big change, even with a plan in place to do so. What if you structured your business so that everyone could work from anywhere at any time? Rather than having to switch gears in the event of a disaster, you could set it up so that your staff can work remotely whenever and wherever necessary. With that type of setup, you have some substantial flexibility when it comes to your workforce. Not only are you able to move your entire staff from the office to remote locations in a short time, but they would already have experience doing so. You also have more options for smaller issues; for instance, what if an employee has a sick child and needs to stay home? No need for them to burn a sick day or for you to scramble to find someone to pick up the slack. They can just work from home. Snowed in? No problem. If you structure your company to be able to work from anywhere you are going to be capable of adapting to disasters big and small on the fly with ease.

4. Don't Cut Corners with Security

Working remotely is a great option and with all the technology available today it can even be easy to implement. As easy as it may seem, do not cut corners with security. As with many things in life, just because something seems easy to do doesn't mean you are doing it correctly. Technology makes a lot of things in our lives easier, but often doing things the easy way makes it easier for the bad guys to take advantage of the situation too.

Some things in business should be left to the professionals. Unless you are an expert in a particular field, you could be doing more harm than good. Saving a couple of bucks in the short term could cost you a lot in the long run. Cybersecurity is a field that falls into this category. While you may be capable of setting up your infrastructure to allow your staff to work remotely, are you able to do it securely?

One major issue I've seen is when companies allow staff to use their personal devices. Because so much of technology is in the cloud these days, all you need is a web browser, right? Why not let employees just use their personal devices? As a business owner, you have no visibility or control over someone's personal devices. They may have inadequate or no virus protection installed. They may have children in the home who use the machine to download pirated video games. They may have an uncle who constantly forwards them every conspiracy theory email he gets. What happens when that personal computer gets a virus that sends everything that the user does back to a hacker? Now that hacker has the credentials to log into your cloud tool. This is just one example. Don't allow personal machines to access anything related to your company. Any cost savings it may provide is not worth the potential issues and liability if something goes wrong.

If you shouldn't allow staff to use personal machines to work remotely, what can you do? In most cases, a company laptop is your best bet. A business-class machine with a professional edition operating system. Docking stations are nice to provide the user with a more desktop-like experience where they work most. With a company machine, you know they have your approved security software, settings, and policies in place.

While many of these will be discussed in further detail throughout this book, here are some important things you should ensure are part of your company computer policies.

- Use multi-factor authentication (MFA) wherever possible, especially with anything that could be accessed from any machine that has an internet connection.

- Have proper password security. Don't allow common or simple passwords just because they are easy to remember. This goes for owners and executives, too. Don't skimp on security just because you're the boss. Chances are that if a hacker got hold of your computer, the outcome would be more catastrophic than anyone else in the company.

- Use a virtual private network connection (VPN), especially if connecting from a public hotspot.

- Make sure hard drives are encrypted so if a device is lost or stolen, the data is protected.

- Limit or restrict the use of external devices such as USB drives to prevent easy theft of data or the introduction of a virus.

- Make sure the operating system locks automatically after a couple of minutes of inactivity. You don't want your employee walking away to make a sandwich and have their child install some virus-infected game while the employee isn't looking.

- Restrict admin rights so no one can install something they shouldn't on the machine. If something needs to be installed, call the IT department to install only approved software.

5. Test, Test, Test!

Now that you have a plan, you are ready for anything, right? Have you tested that plan? Nothing sinks a great plan faster than something you hadn't considered. Testing goes a long way to avoid these types of issues. Here are some common issues I have seen when companies try to have employees work remotely.

Capacity: When a couple of people worked from home, things were fine. When a larger number of people tried connecting to remote resources simultaneously, things slowed to a crawl, or people were unable to log in at all. Make sure that you proactively test capacity. Schedule a day when a group of people can work from home to make sure there are no issues.

Slow Internet Connections: Not everyone has a blazing fast internet connection adequate for working from home, especially if everyone else in their household is stuck at home, too. If the kids are eating up all the bandwidth streaming movies, the productivity of your remote worker is greatly reduced. Make sure your employees have a decent internet connection. Maybe even offer partial reimbursement as an incentive for them to have a better internet plan.

Having the Right Equipment: If someone needs a printer or a scanner to do their job, don't assume they have one at home. Either provide one or offer to pitch in for one they can buy for themselves, but make sure they have one before it's needed. Other common items people seem to be missing when working remotely are webcams and headsets. If you are stuck with your staff working from home, video conferencing is going to be essential. Laptops are notorious for audio issues if you don't have a headset. The last thing you need in a crisis is an employee trying to conference with a customer while the audio is feeding back or going in and out.

By testing periodically with planned remote work, you can alleviate many issues that may arise if a disaster occurs and you are forced to work remotely without warning. Another option is to allow workers regularly to work remotely. Depending on the type of work, many people prove more productive when working remotely on a full or part-time basis. Keeping your workforce flexible will help them react quickly and be more efficient in the face of a crisis.

Keeping your business running smoothly boils down to having a plan, reviewing and updating the plan periodically, and testing the plan regularly. With the proper planning, you'll have your business prepared for any disaster that may strike, from a small fire to a global pandemic. While your competition is scrambling to react, your company will be executing the plan and moving forward.

By the way, if you liked this chapter, you'll LOVE this informative Free Guide on the top 5 things you can do to setup your company to work safely from anywhere. It's titled "The Business Owner's Guide to Working Remotely" and you can grab it for free using the link below.

https://adaptandovercome.getsphinx.com

About the Author

Ryan O'Hara is an entrepreneur, technology professional and founder of Sphinx Technology Solutions, a Cybersecurity and IT service provider in Dearborn, Michigan.

Ryan founded Sphinx in 2009, after working for several years in corporate IT, to bring enterprise-level IT to small and medium-sized businesses. Sphinx has grown from its early service and support roots to become a security-focused managed service provider (MSP), specializing in keeping businesses throughout the United States secure and ready to handle today's rapidly evolving world of cybersecurity.

Ryan can be reached as follows:

Sphinx Technology Solutions

Phone: (313) 482-9930

rohara@spxtech.com

Website: https://sphinx.technology

Do Not Let A Crisis Go to Waste

By Paul Mancuso

Skylar woke up to a phone call from her boss. "We are missing $18,657 out of our corporate checking account." This is a number she would not soon forget as she remembered she had sent that exact amount in a wire transfer a few days prior and the pit in her stomach began to grow. Skylar worked for a small manufacturing company that dealt with high-end parts for performance cars and big rig trucks. It was not an uncommon occurrence for her to wire-transfer large sums of money frequently to material suppliers and vendors. With the onset of the COVID-19 pandemic, her place of employment had made the decision, as did so many others, to move most of the administrative staff to work from home. This decision, though warranted, proved to be a costly decision as the company had just a few weeks prior decided not to upgrade and improve its IT and security infrastructure. In a cost saving measure, this decision caused the company to deplete precious cash reserves at a time they needed them most, and ultimately implement all the security safeguards they had previously declined. This was, of course, after losing the wire transfer and paying for forensics, new computers, and missing precious days of work while waiting for the replacement of the computers and infrastructure to be completed. This could not have happened at a worse time, when every job was important to keeping staff and the business staying open.

Unfortunately, this is just one instance of many companies that have been hit hard not only by the COVID-19 pandemic, but also for under-performing security measures and criminals using that to their advantage in the middle of a worldwide crisis. In this chapter, we will go into seven ways criminals target, manipulate, and attack during times of crisis. This is not limited to COVID-19, but can be anything from hurricanes and natural disasters to supply chain interruptions, medical emergencies, or something as horrific as 9/11 and domestic terrorism. Wired.com online magazine says, "Amid the COVID-19 pandemic, ransomware attacks have increased 148 percent over baseline levels from February 2020."[6]

An unwritten rule for many criminal enterprises is "Do not let a crisis go to waste." This is one of the best times for them to attack and they are very clever at using a crisis to their advantage. You as a business owner should also not let a crisis go to

---

[6]https://www.wired.com/story/opinion-an-unlikely-partner-to-counter-cyberattacks

waste. If you have not addressed your security in your business, now is the time to do so. In the next few pages, we are going to look at seven ways cyber criminals can attack during a crisis and what you can do to help prevent it.

Exploiting Companies with Weak Security

Cyber criminals know that the larger the company they target, the bigger the pay off will be if they successfully hack them. The challenge they face is most often these larger corporations have policies and procedures in place to ensure they have the best cyber security protection and they have the budgets to actually implement it. While some criminals target these types of businesses, the vast majority of them are targeting the smaller companies. Why? They know that they will have a higher success rate because the smaller businesses usually do not have the budgets or knowledge of how to properly secure their business from a cyber security attack. The easier the target, the faster the payday. Criminals know this to be true, therefore they will put effort into targeting a large number of small businesses for a higher number of successful attacks rather than try and get a large corporation that can take months or years to breach. More often than not, small business owners are successfully attacked due to poor password policies and generally a lack of proper security. When a small business experiences an attack, it generally is more inclined to pay a ransom in the case of a ransomware attack because, without paying it, its source of business operation is shut down and the firm is unable to generate revenue. A very common misconception among small business owners is they do not think they have any data that criminals want. In the case of ransomware, which we will detail later, often it is not about the data you have but more about the disruption to your day-to-day business, thus affecting your revenue and making it necessary for you to pay the ransom to get the use of your files back.

COVID-19 caused unprecedented restrictions to be put on businesses and cities all over the world. In a few weeks' time, companies of all sizes transitioned large portions of their staff to a work-from-home workforce. What did that mean for cyber criminals? They now had computers all over the world no longer protected by corporate networks and security policies and now behind consumer home routers and weak security practices. In a short time, cyber crime began to rise as more and more devices were easier to gain access to. COVID-19 was unlike anything the world had ever seen before and criminals shifted quickly to begin targeting new mainstream tools such as Zoom and Microsoft Teams. It began to be a game of chess over hackers finding exploits and companies providing software updates to fix security issues. Almost overnight, tools providing video conferencing, online meetings, and IP phone services all had a huge influx of new users and they had to work around the clock to keep up with demand while keeping ahead of the criminals by patching software. Even before COVID-19, cyber criminals were targeting more and more cloud-based user accounts as ways to gain entry into other networks. Finding weak security practices and standards, hackers were finding it easier than ever to breach accounts and computers. In a very short time, computers and users that were previously protected under a corporate network were now vulnerable and accessible from hundreds of thousands of homes throughout the world. The uncertainty and length of the stay at home orders being unknown made a perfect window of opportunity for criminals to attack. The longer the crisis lasted, the more time companies would have to implement security for their work from home users. Criminals know when to attack, how to mobilize, and how to use a crisis to their advantage. Specifically, they use emotion and opportunity to their advantage.

Opportunity and Emotional Attacks

Being a managed service provider on the gulf coast, we are no strangers to having our customers deal with natural disasters such as hurricanes and severe weather. Any type of crisis can be used by criminals to exploit the emotions of people during times of uncertainty. Two things cyber criminals prey on are opportunity and emotion. They know being in the right place at the right time or having an email sent to the right person at the right time can cause the victim to let his/her guard down and click the link in an email normally considered suspicious, thus giving hackers access to accounts and files to use in a variety of scams. We will go into some specific type of attacks in the next few pages, but I want to cover the mental side of these attacks in this section. Opportunity and emotion are strong tools in the cyber-criminal arsenal, and for good reason: they work.

A crisis such as the recent COVID-19 pandemic was a prime opportunity to run common attacks on victims all over the world at a time where security was more of an afterthought instead of the forefront of most business owners' minds. Many companies were just trying to survive and mobilize their workforce to a work-from-home staff and were not properly executing security plans to go along with this. Criminals knew this and almost immediately began to use news headlines to form websites and emails that were driven on an emotional response from people. In the very early stages of the worldwide pandemic, hackers had already created websites and mobile applications that were said to track the spread of COVID-19 when, in reality, they infected machines with ransomware.[7] They were clearly staying steps ahead of security measures and trying to use the crisis headlines to get people to download these apps and visit the websites. As the virus and shutdowns progressed, the hackers kept changing

---

[7]https://www.helpnetsecurity.com/2020/03/16/fake-covid-19-tracker/

tactics and coming up with new strategies almost daily. They were using every opportunity to execute malicious intent on victims all over the world. As the days and weeks went on, they changed strategies from websites and apps to more personal attacks toward businesses, such as invoice hijacking, email access, and ransomware techniques. The proximity of employees being spread out in a work-from-home labor force proved to be an opportunity that they were able to exploit. No longer was it easy to walk down the hall to verify information directly with a superior, but now they had to rely almost entirely on email communication. The criminals knew this and used techniques to exploit this exact behavior.

In the United States, government officials had passed legislation to give every citizen a stimulus check to help bridge the gap of lost wages due to the closure of the economy due to stay at home orders. Criminals wasted no time using this opportunity and the emotions of people that were financially hurting to try and perpetuate their scams even further. Emails and websites were quickly created to impersonate the government programs and capture people's information for identity theft. They also began using emails looking to be from the United States government loaded with ransomware to encrypt files knowing that people's emotions would make it more likely to open these emails. They were betting on getting an emotional reaction by people that were already uneasy about the uncertainty of finances and the economy. The thought in a criminal's mind is more people will open this email if it is tied to the emotion of them needing that money to survive. It is a horrible practice, but one they use because it is so effective. Remember, they will use opportunity and your emotion every chance they get. Now that we have the general lack of security and the emotions of the victims out of the way, let us look at a few specific tactics used by criminals to exploit these situations.

Brute Force Attack

My father had a saying he would tell me all the time, "Locks are for honest people." Think of your passwords as the keys to the locks of your electronic life. The longer your password, the harder it is to crack (guess) it. When people think of someone trying to hack into their email or computer, they generally think of a person sitting at a computer typing away furiously until they gain access or give up. Often, a hacker is just running a program that is guessing thousands of password combinations across multiple user accounts until gaining access. This is called a brute force attack, where the hacker just simply guesses your password. Most online services are requiring you to have stronger and stronger passwords because of this, but many company policies have not been updated or current policies have not been enforced. When you are coming up with a password policy or even just creating passwords for yourself, remember the following tips.

- Should be a minimum of eight characters in length.

- Should incorporate both upper- and lower-case letters (e.g., a-z and A-Z)

- Should incorporate digits and punctuation characters as well as letters, e.g., 0-9, (! @ # $ % ^ & * ( ) _ - + = { } [ ] : ; " ' | \ / ? < > , . ~ `)

- Should not be words found in a dictionary.

- Should not include easily guessed information such as personal information, names, pets, birth dates, etc.

It may be hard to imagine, but the last one on the list above is critical. If getting into your account is valuable to them, they will look up information on you from social media or Google searches to find things out about you to try and guess your passwords. A brute force attack is a technique used to gain access but what they do after they have access is what is more important. Another technique used is a phishing attack.

Phishing Attack

I am from the state of Louisiana, known as Sportsman's Paradise, and I have always enjoyed fishing. At least I thought I enjoyed fishing until I went on a fishing trip with a boat captain from Cocodrie, La., named "Cuda." He ruined me for fishing. I realized on that trip I enjoy catching fish not the act of fishing as much. "Cuda" is one of the best in the business when it comes to fishing off the coast of Louisiana. He knows the proper techniques, proper bait, and proper location to go from just fishing to catching.

Cyber criminals use a technique called phishing to attack victims and gain access to accounts, and then use that access to their advantage. Just like "Cuda," they know the techniques, the bait, and locations to capture the most "victims." Once they find what works, they use it again. These email scams are constantly evolving as current events change. Remember, they use opportunity and emotion to formulate emails that you will fall for to give up credentials and personal information.

If you are not familiar with what a phishing scam is, it is a technique that criminals use but is not the end goal. Usually a phishing attack is to gain access for them to do more harm at a later date. A hacker will formulate an email, it could be about a current crisis, or some other email you would be inclined to open and read, and have a link in the email for you to click on so they can gain access to an account. For example, a criminal may impersonate Microsoft Office 365 to try and gain access to your email account. If you click on the link, it may go to a page that aesthetically looks exactly like the Microsoft login page. You think nothing of it so you login with your email address and password. It does not actually load your emails but goes to a blank page so you close the browser and go on with your tasks. In fact, the phish is now over and you have given them your login name and password so they can login to your email account. Once they have your password, they can then actually perform other steps to spread the criminal activity further. They are able to read all your email without your knowledge, they can send any emails they want to all of your contacts, they can enable ransomware on your email box, or any other scam they want to run. We have also seen where they will forward all new email to their own email address in case you change your password, they will still get a copy of every email sent to you. Gaining access to your mailbox was just the first step. In the Verizon Wireless 2019 Data Breach Investigation report, 56% of breaches took months or longer to discover. Once the criminals have access, they may monitor your inbox for months to see how you respond to emails, with whom you converse or, in certain cases, use information they discover to perform an invoice hijack.

Invoice Hijacking

We began the chapter with a story about Skylar and the $18,657 lost wire transfer. The events leading up to this were all orchestrated by cyber criminals using a number of the techniques we have already discussed. It began by the criminals executing a phishing attack on Skylar's email. Once she fell for the attack, they began monitoring her email box waiting for the right opportunity and sequence of events to implement an invoice hijacking. It was estimated they were monitoring her email for approximately 2 months before trying to steal the money. This proved to be a huge part of why the scam was successful. The criminals had access to all of her emails so they began to monitor her communication between her and her boss. They noticed patterns in when payments were sent and when bank transfers were done. The name of her boss was also used to create an email account at a domain that was one letter off from the company domain. About a month into monitoring her email, the company made the decision to send administrative staff home due to the COVID-19 crisis. The hackers then waited for the right opportunity with the right dollar amount to make it worthwhile. Skylar received an email from her boss one morning asking her to wire transfer $18,657 to a vendor that they use all the time, but gave her the new routing and account numbers while referencing correct job numbers and PO numbers that they acquired by reading her email for the days and weeks prior. The email was from the fake boss's account that was one letter off from the real domain. Skylar unfortunately did not catch that and because they were working remotely, she was not able to walk into her boss's office to receive further clarification. This type of scam is becoming more and more common as the criminals found it to be more effective while companies transitioned to a work-from-home workforce. In the weeks since the attack, the company has replaced computers and firewall with enterprise equipment that also includes a full security stack that covers email and URL protection. They also put a policy and procedure in place having physical checks and balances on wire transfers and customer account changes. A large area they found that needed to be addressed was simply training for the employees on cyber security best practices. Working on policies and procedures internally is just as important as the software you use to keep you secure. Cybercrime does not appear to be going away any time soon and a crisis seems to intensify the threats in frequency and in scope of damage.

Ransomware

If you have not heard of ransomware or cryptocurrency, hopefully we can shed some light on what it is and how it can affect you. To start, Webster's dictionary defines cryptocurrency as any form of currency that only exists digitally, that usually has no central issuing or regulating authority, but instead uses a decentralized system to record transactions and manage the issuance of new units. Essentially, it is an untraceable currency that cannot be linked back to an individual easily. Cryptocurrency is the currency of choice for cybercriminals, especially those who distribute ransomware to their victims. Ransomware is defined as malware that requires the victim to pay a ransom to access encrypted files. These two things combined make the perfect solution for a criminal to use to his advantage.

Ransomware is usually distributed through a link in an email that will bring you to a site to download a file, an email attachment that is infected, or from a website made to look like a well-known site that would confuse victims into thinking it was legitimate. Once you have infected your machine with Ransomware, it will begin encrypting all of your files on your computer, network shares, and certain variations also have the ability to encrypt cloud services like Office 365 and Dropbox. The reason this is an effective technique used by criminals is many organizations believe that the most cost-effective way to get their data back is to just pay the ransom. The problem is, right now, that may actually be the case. When business owners pay the ransom, they are not only getting their files back, but also funding development of new ransomware as well as embolden the criminals to attack again. Cybersecurity Ventures estimates that these attacks will cost the global economy nearly $6 trillion annually by 2021.[8]

In the event of a crisis like COVID-19, many companies would not have the cash reserves to recover from or security in place to prevent a ransomware attack, and unfortunately many would have to close their doors. Part of your responsibility as a business owner is to make sure you have a security plan in place that you can mobilize your workforce and work safely and securely so you are able not just to survive during a

---

[8] https://cybersecurityventures.com

crisis, but thrive on the other side of it. Your cyber security plan should be just as important as your physical security plan.

Physical Security

When you think of cyber security you do not usually think of physical locks and alarms for your brick and mortar business, but it is just as important in times of crisis. You should have a security plan in place that restricts access to any server or network closets as well as your physical building. Monitored alarms and camera security is also highly recommended.

During a crisis, if your business must transition to work from home quickly, your physical building will likely not be occupied for days or weeks at a time. During the COVID-19 shutdown, offices were closed for 1-3 months or longer depending on local regulations. Your physical security also needs to be a part of your cyber security plan. The following best practices would not apply to all businesses equally but, as a rule, it is best to follow these guidelines for physical security access.

- Have a separate room for network and server equipment.

- Do not let this room be used for storage.

- Have a camera system on all external doors and in the server room.

- Have an alarm on the main building and a separate alarm system on the server room.

- Have controlled and logged access to the physical server equipment.

Making sure you have logged access for the server or network room means you know who has access to the physical server at all times and that information is logged. Having cameras with motion sensors is also a great feature to have because you can be alerted on your smart phone any time motion is detected. In the event of a crisis where physical access to the building is not possible, you can monitor access from your phone and report any suspicious activities to the authorities. No matter what technique, attack, or physical breaches you encounter, they all should be part of a larger comprehensive cyber security plan.

Comprehensive Cyber Security Plan

COVID-19 was not the first crisis that the business community faced, and it certainly will not be the last. While it was unprecedented, what we learn from it and implement in our businesses is what is most important. If you found you were not prepared for COVID-19, what are you doing to prepare for the next uncertainty in your business? The only thing for certain is we will face uncertainty again. Cyber criminals are not afraid to use opportunity and emotion to attack you, your business, or your employees. How you prepare and respond now will determine if you survive the next crisis you face. Now is not the time to be reactive, you need to start being proactive in your approach to security, your ability to have employees work from anywhere, and training them on best cyber security practices. At a minimum, your cyber security plan should include the following.

- Cloud-Based Email Solution
- Video Conferencing Plan
- Cloud File Server
- Multi-Factor Authentication
- Disaster and Recovery Plan
- Desktop and Email Backups
- Password Policies
- Cloud Phone System
- Enterprise Router with VPN capability
- Ongoing Dark Web Scanning
- Employee Cyber Security Training
- Password Management Program

The above is a general checklist and not all inclusive. My recommendation is to find a company that specializes in security to walk you through the process. Not all MSPs are the same and you need to work with one that you trust and that is focused first and foremost on your security.

Kyle Ardoin, Secretary of State for Louisiana, in a speech to the National Association of Secretaries of State said, "As attacks grow more sophisticated, many MSPs have not been upfront with their clients about the need to invest more in security" He went on to say, "It's not about saving money, it's about protecting systems."

As a business owner, you will need to embrace technology and embrace security. As the leader in your business, you need to take the lead in learning and utilizing technology and security platforms. It must be engrained in the DNA of your business. Security needs to be a core value and that starts with the business owner and leadership team. Be the example for your employees. If you were not prepared for the most recent crisis, do not let a crisis go to waste and make sure you are prepared for the next one.

About the Author

Paul Mancuso is the President and CEO of Vital Integrators based out of Lafayette, LA. Vital Integrators currently has 10 staff members and has customers along the Gulf Coast from Texas to Florida. Paul has a unique perspective and understanding of the IT industry as a Managed Service Provider but also installs and designs audio, video, and lighting systems for churches and businesses that have a strong desire to integrate those systems around a core IT infrastructure. He desires to provide a personal and accurate service to clients by helping both businesses and end users fully utilize technology to enhance day to day operations.

Paul excels in the field of network and systems integration, as well as managing corporate networks. He specializes in finding better, more efficient, and more creative ways of accomplishing goals, which frequently prove to be more cost-effective. He is extremely motivated by the challenge of helping to redirect the course of an organization through the proper use of technology, and he takes great satisfaction in helping them save money in the process. Paul resides in Lafayette, LA with his wife Misty and sons Landon and Greyson.

If you need guidance in coming up with a comprehensive cyber security plan or need to have a cyber security assessment done, visit vitalsecurityexperts.com to set up an appointment or contact Paul Mancuso below:

Office: 337-313-4200

Website: vitalsecurityexperts.com

Social Media: @vitalintegrators

Do Not Feed the PHISH

By Matt Taylor

Doesn't it usually start with that one email from someone's assistant? They open some email that usually goes along the lines of "We have detected unusual activity..." or "Please review your recent Sign-in activity..." or "Your password will expire soon..." or "Please update your payment details..." and they click the big shiny colored button somewhere in the email.

Now, whoever is opening this email is on a webpage and asked to enter their username and password for one of their specific services – this could be Microsoft Office 365, Netflix, DocuSign, etc. This user was just "Phished".

phish·ing /'fiSHiNG/ noun

"The fraudulent practice of sending emails purporting to be from reputable companies to induce individuals to reveal personal information, such as passwords and credit card numbers."

"An email that is likely a phishing scam"

Now that I have officially brought you up to speed what phishing is - the damage is done. The alarms should start blaring, except they do not. Very few users realize what they had just done and typically this starts as a silent attack. As time goes on, things start to slowly change, your actual password does change to your service, a cybercriminal impersonates you, your account is banned or deleted. One of the worst ways to find out you have been phished, is to get multiple phone calls or emails from other business contacts, this could be co-workers, contacts at other businesses. Either way it is not great call or email to receive.

Today in Year 2020, IT is NOT simple, it is rather complex and will only grow in its complexity. There are too many variables to give a definitive answer to what actually happened. Typically, once a person received this type of information, their next call is to their IT Department. Remember those alarms I referenced – are now silently going off inside all the minds of the IT staff. The next step is some sort of investigative process. The IT Department will start rectifying your account in your company and start diving in to find out what happened. How many others this spread to; notify other users in your company, notify others and their IT Department at other companies.

Depending on how big the spread was, it could be a very long cycle for everyone involved to investigate what and how much damage was done.

I have seen the damage firsthand and the effects it has against companies. At the end of the day, it just becomes extremely expensive very quick. I was brought in for an investigation of Office 365 for a division of a company that is very well known around the world. In short, either the user was phished or had a weak password that was ultimately compromised and cybercriminals impersonated that user, sent the appropriate contact for a vendor an email asking for bank account information to be updated, next thing was that the vendor changed the bank account information and wired over 100k.

I have also been involved in several ransomware cases and have seen how costly business interruptions, staff, and consultants to advise or work restoring backups, etc. At a minimum, any type of cyberattack could impact businesses for a few hours up to several days/weeks/months and all at a cost. Depending on the severity – some businesses have closed permanently or downsized significantly.

Cyber Attacks are constantly rising and are expected to cost companies over $8 trillion over the next 5 years.[9] There is no possible way to line up every different type of Cyber Attack out there. During this day and age, hopefully you have

---

[9] https://www.cyberdefensemagazine.com/how-to-train-your-staff-on-cyber-security

already heard of some of these terms and if not, I am glad you are reading this book.

There are only two logical paths - either your business has been impacted or you are looking for ways to help prevent cyberattacks from happening to their business.

The typical IT staff structure is as follows: Small Business are anywhere from 1-3 IT staff and may or may not have an IT Service Provider; Medium Business are anywhere from 1-20+ IT staff and may or may not have an IT Service Provider; Large/Enterprise Business are anywhere from 1-20+ IT staff that consist of multiple teams and divisions and could have a mix of actual employees and contractors/consultants.

Small and Medium Business IT staff ultimately try to perform all the IT roles themselves for various reasons. Users are the biggest problem and the weakest link in cyber security as they make mistakes. These mistakes might include clicking on suspicious links, opening unknown email attachments, using the same passwords – these common errors are the result of a lack of training and security awareness.

Security Awareness Training is a formal process for educating employees about computer security. A good security awareness program should educate employees about policies and procedures for working with IT. They should know who to contact if they discover a threat, how to be aware of phishing attempts. Depending on what type of IT security and control policies your company wants to utilize as a guideline for IT, there could be different criteria that would need to have implemented.

There was a time that IT was responsible for IT, and that was that. Unfortunately, with Technology expanding and growing more complex, all employees (IT or non-IT) must be a part of the solution. Now the time for Business and IT executives to be responsible make sure the business is protected in every aspect of IT. If your staff is unaware of the latest types of cyberattacks and basic rules of information security, then your company is practically powerless and extremely vulnerable to data breaches. Honestly, if an employee touches a computer, they need cybersecurity training.

So, what is next?

To minimize carless cybersecurity mistakes and encourage employee vigilance – you should talk with your employees about cybersecurity at least once a month. Security issues should always be on the top of your employees' minds. Inform your staff about the latest techniques and penetration methods that cybercriminals use. Employees should know what potential impact a breach could have on a company and on each staff member separately.

According to the Verizon 2020 Data Breach Report[10]:

- 22% of breaches involved Phishing
- 28% of breaches involved small business victims
- 58% of victims had Personal data compromised
- Over 80% of breaches within cyberattacks involve Brute force of the Use of lost or stolen credentials

An effective method of training employees is a faux phishing attack. This method will help train employees on how to recognize and handle emails that may contain dangerous links and attachments. Do not forget to include the importance of strong passwords in your cybersecurity training. Passwords must be complicated. Even well-educated cybersecurity specialists tend to make mistakes – so all staff should be involved in constant training including IT professionals, CEOs, and CISOs. Top managers are especially vulnerable as they typically have access to confidential data and IT staff is a key target because of their administrative access to all networks and resources. Cybercriminals with the intention to intrude corporate networks often know who the executives are which means company management are even more at risk.

---

[10]https://enterprise.verizon.com/resources/reports/2020/2020-data-breach-investigations-report.pdf

In additional to routine risk assessments, your staff need to be tested and assessed. You should know their level of knowledge and skills to identify gaps. For example, perform fake phishing attacks to see how many employees will click on those suspicious links and consequently provide information. For those who fell for the fake phishing emails - conduct additional training create multiple courses and workshops. You may also see how many employees will transmit confidential company data over email if asked on a website or service.

Companies should constantly conduct security awareness training and include practical examples of the more common security threats and vulnerabilities. Employees must have a clear understanding that ignorance, carelessness, and unwillingness to study will invariably lead to constant data losses and cybercriminals' attacks.

Creating an effective cybersecurity training starts at the top, is meaningful, and ongoing. According to Edgepoint Learning, here are some tips to help:[11]

Executive Buy-in

Play with the numbers – the costs of security awareness training are worth it when protecting your customers, their data and your company's proprietary information.

---

[11] https://www.edgepointlearning.com/blog/cyber-security-training

Find the Weakest Points in Your System

Do you have gaps in your company's security? Look at all the overall security already in place and then consider the weakest points in your system. Focus the start of your course design there.

Figure Out What Employees Already Know

Do not waste employees' time teaching them what they already know. Work on evaluating individual employee awareness before sending to everyone to the same training.

Capture Learning Opportunities

Do not reinvent the wheel. Chances are good that your company already has some training resources at hand. If your employees respond better to online training, do not force them into a room and bore them with a presentation. Capture as much feedback on the training itself from as many employees as possible.

Concentrate on Phishing Scams

Even the most well-informed employees may not be completely up to date on every scam that comes out. Teach employees how to protect the company and themselves. Nearly 91% of cyberattacks start with an email.

Standardize Company-Wide Password Policies

What should be the criteria for each password? Capital letter? Special character? Eight or more characters? Two factor authentication?

SET THE STANDARD!

Make sure the entire company knows what it is and create automatic processes that force them force them to update their passwords.

Use Personal Examples

In a company of any size, chances are good that at least one employee have been the victim of some form of identity theft or cyberattack. Make it personal. Get (willing) employees share their experiences – tying them back to protecting the company. Everyone is vulnerable.

Make it Real-Time

Create simulated cyberattacks. These training exercises can strengthen security awareness and prepare for the real deal.

Train Early, Train Often

Start security awareness training during the onboarding process as an integral part of joining the company. This will assist identifying new employees' level of awareness and tailor to their needs.

Make it an Ongoing Team Effort

Security Awareness Training should be an ongoing, team effort that takes in changes in the industry, the world, and the ever-changing tools used during cyberattacks. Organizations tend roll out an annual training and think it is one and done. Not exactly. Your employees are your company's assets. Invest in them. Just like your computer or any other hardware or software – if you do not continuously stay updated, you will remain open to vulnerabilities.

So, you - as an Owner, CEO, Executive – have a decision to make. Are you going to be irresponsible and not invest in your staff or are you going to protect your company and ensure proper Security Awareness is executed?

How Much RISK Are You Willing to Accept?

About the Author

Matt Taylor is the founder and CEO of Darkside Enterprises, a national managed solution provider. Matt is a seasoned IT Professional and has spent the last 15 years implementing multiple IT and Cyber Security Solutions for hundreds of organizations across various industries. Matt is passionate and committed to serving his clients and offering the best in class solutions to advance their technology within their organization. He also holds multiple certifications with Microsoft & CompTIA, CEH, CRISC, CISM, CISSP, CCSP, PMP, PMI Risk Management Professional, Six Sigma Green Belt, Lean Sigma Green Belt.

When not absorbed by work, you can find Matt with his beautiful wife and six kids – typically building massive Star Wars or Superhero LEGO Sets or movies. He is active in his kid's school community and enjoys family vacations.

May the force will be with you.

If you are not sure where to start, I would encourage you to join us for our Cyber Security Awareness Webinar. Register to find out the best practices for security awareness for your industry!

Register at https://CSAT1.darksidemsp.it today.

Follow us on Facebook and LinkedIn:

https://www.facebook.com/darksideenterprisesinc

https://www.linkedin.com/company/darkside-enterprises-inc

How to Keep Your Data Secure & Safe During a Crisis

By Chee Lam

You might remember the Northeast blackout of 2003, a widespread power outage that shut down power generation, water supply, transportation, communication, and various industries throughout parts of the Northeastern and Midwestern U.S., and Toronto, Canada, where I live. All our clients' systems and data survived.

You might also recall the 2010 G20 Toronto summit riot as a group of protesters caused vandalism to businesses in downtown Toronto. More than 20,000 police, military, and security personnel were involved shutting down access to the downtown core. Not only did our clients' systems and data survive, but employees were able to continue working remotely and securely.

Fast forward to the year 2020 today, with the COVID-19 pandemic resulting in millions of cases and hundreds of thousands of deaths worldwide. This most contagious virus has negatively affected the livelihoods and the global economy since it first emerged. It caused severe global socioeconomic disruptions, from producers, supply chain, tourism, retail sector, and air travel to local small businesses, and offices to be closed. Drastic measures have been implemented, such as travel curbs, border controls, and countrywide lockdowns.

Our team worked around the clock responding to every crisis while keeping all our clients' systems running securely and safely, both on-premises and in the cloud. How did we do it? Let us explore further.

Data is the new currency

"In a digital economy, data is the new currency exchanged between consumers and businesses. It is a resource that is often unseen but carries monumental consequences if left unsecured," said RSA Director of Digital Risk Solutions, Angel Grant, and National Cyber Security Alliance (NCSA) Executive Director, Kelvin Coleman.

"More than one-quarter of businesses say that unmanaged risks would have a negative consequence on their customer relationships and could also impact brand reputation, future viability and regulatory compliance," they further added in their joint NCSA blog post.[12]

---

[12]https://staysafeonline.org/blog/digital-transformation-are-you-risk-ready/

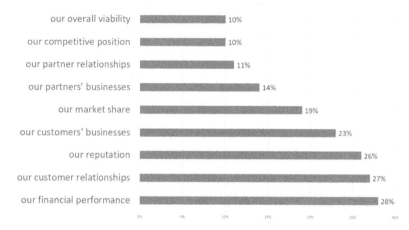

Figure A: Risk Consequences

From inside attackers, state-backed sophisticated hackers, to your neighbors, cybercriminals are among us. It is even more prevalent during crises as we usually see a huge uptake in cybercriminal reconnaissance activities. Take the most recent pandemic for example; COVID-19 related cyber attacks spiked 400%. Online crimes reported to the FBI's Internet Crime Complaint Center IC3 (the main ingestion point) have quadrupled from 1,000 to 4,000 complaints daily.[13]

All these crises share the same downside in the digital world in which we live; they deliver an extraordinary array of cybersecurity challenges. You may be reading this at your comfort, but I can attest your IT department, CISO, security consultants, and MSPs are working hard every

[13]https://thehill.com/policy/cybersecurity/493198-fbi-sees-spike-in-cyber-crime-reports-during-coronavirus-pandemic

second keeping your business safe and secure. Some businesses may not be fortunate and many of them caught in an "epidemic" of crisis of its own are either being forced to scale down, declare bankruptcy, or permanently close.

Each crisis provides the breeding ground and opportunity for cybercriminals to prey on common people to the point where we read the news of data breaches compromising personal information of millions of people around the world everyday. It is a perfect storm. According to IBM,[14] data breaches were costing companies USD $3.92 million per incident in 2019, impacting an average of 25,575 records. In the same year alone, the U.S. tops the chart as the most expensive country with USD $8.19 million per breached incident. Unless you live in a cave, chances are you have heard about at least one of these breaches.

Company	Date	Impact
Lifelabs	October 2019	15 million user records
Adobe	October 2013	153 million user records
Adult Friend Finder	October 2016	412.2 million accounts
Canva	May 2019	137 million user accounts

---

[14] https://www.ibm.com/security/data-breach

eBay	May 2014	145 million users
Equifax	July 29 2017	147.9 million consumers
LinkedIn	2012 and 2016	165 million user accounts
Marriot	2014-2018	500 million customers
Sina Weibo (China's Twitter)	March 2020	538 million accounts
Yahoo!	2013-2014	3 billion user accounts

Figure B: Breach examples.[15]

Regional breach Lifelabs looks seemingly outnumbered compared to other historical breaches. However, those 15 million records represent over 40% of Canadians. Not only was ransom paid, Lifelabs also was faced with a proposed $1.13 billion class action lawsuit.[16] The compromised database included health card numbers, names, email addresses, logins, passwords, dates of birth, and lab test results. Even though ransom was paid, there is no guarantee the cybercriminals will abide by their word not to resell

[15]https://www.csoonline.com/article/2130877/the-biggest-data-breaches-of-the-21st-century.html
[16]https://www.canadianunderwriter.ca/insurance/lifelabs-facing-proposed-class-action-lawsuit-over-data-breach-1004172297/

information on the dark web. Breaches like this do not need to occur twice for your identity to be compromised elsewhere in the digital world. It is a matter of time, not if.

What is Data Security?

Data security refers to ways of protecting digital data from destructive forces and from unwanted actions of unauthorized users, such as cyberattacks or a data breach.[17] In other words, they are measures taken to protect your data such as the information in QuickBooks, your banking information, customer information like credit card and social insurance numbers or social security numbers, business and trade secrets, or intellectual property. Your data can exist in the cloud, server, desktop, laptop, or mobile device, both in transit or at rest among all users within your company – pretty much everything that lives inside digital devices.

Data security is also commonly referred to as information security, IT security, or computer security, and is an integral part of the information technology eco-system for organizations of all sizes, large or small.

---

[17] https://en.wikipedia.org/wiki/Data_security

What is Data Security Trying to Protect?

The information security landscape is constantly changing such that my security presentation to our clients is never the same. In fact, it evolves so rapidly that we are sometimes asked about new threats that we haven't even heard about yet. Below are some of the ways used by cybercriminals to obtain your data:

Figure C: Threat types

Imagine keeping track and learning each of them; it would be overwhelming to most business owners. Although these are important security perimeter considerations when designing your overall security architecture, it is entirely a topic of its own for another day. Nonetheless, we can categorically put them all into three consistent threat buckets:

i. **Security Hackers:** People who work to exploit vulnerabilities in computer systems.

ii. **Malware:** A broad term used to describe all sorts of malicious software, including viruses, and may have a variety of goals. Malware can include viruses, spyware, trojans, worms, nagware, keyloggers, etc.

iii. **Computer viruses:** A form of malware designed to replicate and spread.

According to McAfee, the terms "virus" and "malware" are often used interchangeably. However, they are technically different, so the question of malware vs. viruses is, technically, an important one.[18]

To put these three in context, a hacker would collaborate and use variants of malware to infect computers using viruses as an effective agent exploiting vulnerabilities to the masses in the shortest time possible. In terms of scalability, this is an effective way to build "qualified" victims through automation.

Techniques used by hackers

There are three principal broad techniques used by hackers:

i. Password Spray

---

[18]https://www.mcafee.com/enterprise/en-ca/security-awareness/ransomware/malware-vs-viruses.html

Brute-force: An attacker submitting many passwords with the hope of eventually guessing correctly. With credentials sold on the dark web, guessing the other portion of your password is now closer than you think.

   ii.   Breach Replay

Dark web trades: Hackers also use information sold in the dark web to gain unauthorized access. They buy and sell information such as email addresses, usernames, and passwords.

   iii.   Phishing

Phishing through email: Also known as business email compromise (BEC), it is when victims are sent an email purported to be from someone with whom they regularly communicate, such as their boss or a supplier. Sometimes it could appear to be from a system-generated email and often contains an urgent request for payment, money or wire transfer or change of banking details.

Over the years, we collected and have seen some interesting and creative ways of phishing. One BEC was with a voice message attachment and, upon execution, it would alter and create an Outlook rule to forward all email communication and delete itself to avoid detection. Cybercriminals will then capture all communication and "study" the victim and its organization (reconnaissance) before launching a highly effective targeted attack.

Phishing through phone call: Also known as voice phishing (vishing). With access to a phone database acquired illegally, the hacker poses as a business, or more typically a bank or government organization, and calls the victim to obtain personal information for financial gain and threatens to law enforcement if the victim does not comply.

Phishing through text messages: Also known as SMS phishing (smishing). As with email, the phishing victim would receive a text message with a link instead claiming to be from a government authority. This fraudulent SMS is attempting to trick victim into believing he/she has received a government benefit or tax refund. Once submitting the login credentials through the malicious website, hackers would then assume your identity for financial gain.

Why Data Security Is So Difficult To Do

Today's technology resiliencies can survive, with proper planning, almost any type of catastrophe or crisis. In fact, data security is thriving and becoming more resilient and widely adopted with the advent of cloud computing. As a result, ubiquitous computing and convergence have greatly influenced our daily life and made it so easy for us to connect, communicate, and share data. These digital conveniences and innovations are both a blessing and a curse as they present an equal opportunity for cybercriminals.

There are so many tools I can show you to get the job done. However, without the understanding of why data security is failing for so many, the tools will be likely a band-aid and a costly solution for you.

Examples of Common Concerns From the Field

Throughout my consulting practice helping many clients and peers, some of them relate to productivity to get the job done at the expense of security whilst other relate to human nature, ignorance, and negligence, or simply downplaying the risk because it costs them money. Some of the common concerns below are field examples when talking to clients about what they think about their data security protection:

- Do not understand how data is protected and how can be better protected.

- Internal risk from unauthorized access, use, and transmit data to external.

- Limited knowledge of what type of data they own, where it is stored, how sensitive it might be, or if it is subject to regulatory/ compliance requirement and the risk of unauthorized access.

- No visibility of data security for remote workers or contractors through VPN, file sharing, or email.

- Freedom and flexibility of work culture resulting in a loosely written digital use policy by entrusting employees to do their own due diligence.

- Uncategorized, unindexed, unstructured, and widely dispersed data, making it difficult to track, search, monitor, and protect.

- It is not a priority.

- Overly reliant on specific controls to protect data, such as device encryption over everything else.

- Status-quo or catering to one part of network or platform without considering all areas: iOS/ Android ignoring Windows, or continuing to perimeter firewall-based models because that is what was approved.

Do any of the above reflect your situation or make you uncomfortable? Is your data as secure as you think it is? I thought so, please indulge me and read further.

Evolution of Data Security

There used to be a basic checklist to get a firewall, router, switches, and cables to secure your own perimeter. While it is still essential (I call it the **old world**), it has become increasingly irrelevant in many cases today. Explosion of the connected world means more collaboration with apps and people where cloud computing proves to be low cost, effective, and agile to businesses (the **new world**). The paradigm shifts with COVID-19 pandemic, where the entire world population has been forced to work remotely, has just accelerated the adoption. Therefore, we must evolve alongside with how cybercriminals operate to protect our data effectively.

Old World vs. New World	
Full-time employees	Gig economy with outsourced contractors, employees on-demand, partners, and customers
Full blown on-premise applications	Explosion of cloud apps offering low cost, modular subscription model
Corporate-owned devices	Bring your own devices
Corporate network and firewall	Cloud first, mobile first borderless internetworks
Local packet tracking and data logging	Explosion of security signals beyond corporate security perimeter

Figure D: Old world vs. New world

Meet Cybercrime-as-a-Service

"China's cybercrime enterprise is large, lucrative, and expanding quickly," Anne An reported in her blog post at McAfee.[19] She continued to say, "According to 2018 Internet Development

---

[19] https://www.mcafee.com/blogs/other-blogs/mcafee-labs/how-chinese-cybercriminals-use-business-playbook-to-revamp-underground/

Statistics, China's cybercriminal underground was worth more than US $15 billion, nearly twice the size of its information security industry. The same Chinese-language source also shows that China's cybercrime is growing at a rate of more than 30 percent a year. An estimated 400,000 people work in underground cybercriminal networks."

"With regard to hacking services, Chinese cybercriminals also offer modules for prospective clients to fill out their service requests, including types of attacks, target IP addresses, desirable malware or exploit toolkits, and online payment processing," Anne An further stated. It is therefore an entire industry itself and is here to stay.

Can I have social engineering with cherry on top please? It is already established where you can order your favorite attack *a la carte,* tailored to your budget and goal. The advent of cybercrime-as-a-service or attacks-as-a-service driven by sophisticated organized cybercriminals has transformed the threat landscape of data security, including the way it is protected.

Evolution of data security threats

Figure E: Data Security Threat Evolution

The Difference Between Data Security and Privacy

Often, when I speak to business owners, the word *security* and *privacy* are constantly intertwined and become confused. It is important to distinguish the difference between the two. Although they are closely intertwined, privacy shapes and dictates the handling of data whilst data security defines controls that are in place to protect data. For example, your organization can meet regulatory requirements and audit controls pertaining to keeping data secure. But it can still collect, use, track, and disclose personal client information during commercial business to the extent that your clients may believe it violates their privacy.

The Solution

Data security issues have become so problematic we should rethink how we protect our data. Gone is the *old world* of firewalling and rules. Crisis over crisis, my team demonstrated a solid strategy to secure data for what I call a 3-part framework that will change the way you talk about data security and perhaps the way you protect them in the *new world*. My advice: do not skip the steps.

The 3-Part Framework

1. Make Data Security Risk Management a Business Enabler

2. The Perfect Data Security

3. Drive strategic outcomes with context driven security program

1. Make Data Security Risk Management a Business Enabler

Without you championing your data security initiative as an important agenda item, no one will. Even if you hire a security professional, your solution will be half-baked. Why? Because navigating through IT technology, policies, and solutions is not a straight path. Business leaders and executives must believe that data security is so important, as if your business survival depends on it in the *new world*.

Just like building physical structures, physical security is embedded and part of architectural design. Technology adoption should be no different with data security. You, as a business leader or member of the board, must include data security as part of the conversation with your IT department, MSP, or security consultant. It is okay not to understand what an APT[20] or file-less memory attack is. Be supportive and open-minded to your IT advisors and try to understand the impact by quantifying the risk in terms of dollars and cents.

2. The Perfect Data Security

As I mentioned in the Evolution of Data Security, cybercriminals are constantly improving and evolving. Do not think for a second that your data security is adequate and perfect. There is no such thing as perfect data security. If cybercriminals are working hard to break you, it is time for us to up our game and be vigilant – NOW. Allocate a data security budget – OPEX or CAPEX? I will leave that up to your CFO.

"How much should I allocate?" you might ask. There is no hard-and-fast rule, as it depends on your risk tolerance (what is acceptable and not), your industry (regulated or not), company size, and your overall IT budget vs revenue. If you are in a regulated financial vertical, as are most of my financial clients, I recommend an average 10% of the total IT spend or about $2,300 per full-time employee. These numbers represent an average

---

[20] https://en.wikipedia.org/wiki/Advanced_persistent_threat

0.3% of total revenue. This guidance comes from the Deloitte Center for Financial Services analysis survey, which is very much aligned to all my clients' spending today for a healthy data security program in place.

Average cybersecurity spending range at financial institutions (overall sample)

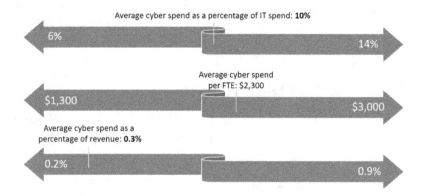

Figure F: 2019 FSISAC/Deloitte Cyber Risk Services CISO Survey[21]

It is also worth noting that the average amount spent per employee is the same between small and medium-sized companies. Understandably, the amount is higher for large companies due to the higher cost of acquisition because there are more processes and operating costs in place to provide the solution. We can see the amount also has a larger impact on small businesses, with

[21]https://www2.deloitte.com/us/en/insights/industry/financial-services/cybersecurity-maturity-financial-institutions-cyber-risk.html

twelve percent (12%) to their bottom line whereas both mid-size and large fared at nine percent (9%).

The point is, it <u>does not matter</u> if you are a small Chartered Professional Accountant (CPA) shop, healthcare provider, or multinational corporation. To have solid data security protection, the amount spent is almost identical. Essentially, it takes the same amount of resources to run a data security program because cybercriminals really run the gamut, regardless of their target, big or small; it is the data that matters.

Financial institutions' average cybersecurity spending, by company size

	Small	Midsize	Large
Cyber spend as a percentage of IT spend	12%	9%	9%
Cyber spend per FTE	$2,100	$2,100	$2,700
Cyber spend as a percentage of revenue	0.2%	0.5%	0.9%

Figure G: 2019 FSISAC/Deloitte Cyber Risk Services CISO Survey[22]

3. Drive strategic outcomes with context-driven security programs

Consider the following: Uber, Airbnb, Slack, Trello, Zapier, etc. Of all these SaaS tools, which one did you most recently install? Maybe it was Intralinks or Firmex for a virtual data room, or Expensify for your mobile workforce, possibly along with a

[22]https://www2.deloitte.com/us/en/insights/industry/financial-services/cybersecurity-maturity-financial-institutions-cyber-risk.html

custom app to connect to an outsourced fund administrator. How can we maintain productivity with these 3rd party apps while protecting ourselves from the data being maliciously used? For full peace of mind, you need a context-driven security solution.

We need automated policy monitoring and enforcement to help us gain more visibility into these attack surfaces. We also need an automated and integrated toolset to give us agile and efficient threat protection. This solution needs to be able to automatically classify and tag documents throughout its lifecycle, to protect intellectual property and regulated data.

When we shift our thinking and take this approach, we stop asking questions like, "What data do I need to protect?" Instead, we focus more on strategic questions like:

- What applications are trying to gain access to my environment and who are the users doing this?

- Why, when and where are they requesting the data?

- What data are they requesting?

- What is the likelihood that the application activity is malicious?

- Can we detect and prevent malicious activities automatically?

Do you see how these questions have shifted from only focusing on protecting data to bigger security concerns? We are now looking at things such as who has access and how we can protect everything we need to protect. These aspects of security are just like the examples of common concerns from the field stated earlier, which are all valid points but which all are focusing mainly on data itself. We are seeing data security with tunnel vision and undoubtedly we often question why data security is difficult to achieve.

When I speak to 'C' level executives and partners, there is often a big gap between their understanding of what they think their data security program does, and the reality of the one in place in their company. The explosion of the interconnected digital world, huge numbers of devices and myriad security programs has made this whole subject complicated and confusing.

So, where should you start? Ask your team and yourself honestly; how mature is your security program? This should not be about how much you spent, but how it compares to your industry peers.

- What coverage do you have with your current security setup? Is it comprehensive enough in the ***new world***?

- Where are you at today with your data security?

- Where do you want to be with it and what is your goal?

When planning for data security program that truly suits your needs, I recommend *shooting for the stars*; that way, at least if anything falls short, you still have the moon so to speak. Start by having an overarching data security plan and a comprehensive roadmap of how to put that plan into place. Quantify and calculate the risk in dollars and cents. Typically, efficiency ratio and ROI are the main aspects of a discussion. However, how data security is planned, executed, and governed is as important, if not more so, than the cost, in order to ensure continuity of the program.

"So where do I start again?" I get it. This is not your cup of tea, and it should not have to be because you have better things to do. Just like a CPA trying to educate me about the concept of compound interest, no matter how simple it is my brain just shuts down. For that reason, I suggest speaking to peers who have had success with security implementation procedures. Take the time to understand these, so that your team will:

- Understand the current state of security controls in place

- Develop a practical security goal

- Be able to have clear roadmap and set milestones to achieve your security goal

- Be able to understand how your organization culture, people, processes, and business partners need to adapt to new security initiatives

There is no perfect security solution as the digital world continues to evolve. There is also no quick deployment or set-it-forget-it security solution. I truly believe that to embrace digital trans-formation, we need to look at intelligence and automation where machine learning and A.I. are the core competencies of the solution. The ***new world*** requires a new approach and ideally covers the four areas below:

1. Identity Access Management (IAM)

2. Cloud Security

3. Information Protection

4. Threat Protection

Keep in mind that not all security programs are created equal. Ask and make sure the solution meets the ***new world*** requirements. Here at my company, I call our solution **FORTIFY +1**.

Contextual Security with FORTIFY +1

Identity Access Management	Cloud Security	Information Protection	Threat Protection
Ensure only the right people have the right access to organizational resources.	Gain end-to-end visibility of security and compliance across clouds and applications, including shadow IT.	Protect documents, databases, and emails against leaks, tampering of evidence, and destruction.	Stop and remove hackers and recover instantly during an attack.

Remember I mentioned about not all security programs being created equal? Well, there is that +1 that sets us apart.

Summary

People ask me how to keep their data secure and safe during a crisis. I often reply, "This should not be just during a crisis." It may have been a relevant question two decades ago in the *old world*. It is not the case today, when data security is no longer an accessory but an essential tool for the protection of our daily lives. Individuals, corporations, and countries that can harvest the greatness of technology wisely will boom; those that make bad or no technology choices will collapse and disappear.

Do not wait until tomorrow, because the threat-scape is changing every second. Everyone must view data security as a business enabler from the start. In the **new world** today, every day is a crisis day.

About the Author

Chee Lam's career spanned multi disciplines in IT. During his 25 years of an IT career, he worked for both corporate end user's IT and as IT consultant for MSP serving clients before starting his company in 2016. Once an outsourced Microsoft employee, he served high-profile clients such as the U.S. military, British High Commission, and Fortune 500 companies. He then joined ING Direct Bank, where he was heading the bank's email system and mobile devices division's security program. In 2015, he joined a fintech start-up, ZenBanx, where he ran its global command center headquartered in Toronto, with regional offices in Wilmington, Delaware and San Francisco, California.

As a founder and CEO of Deskflix Inc. in Toronto, Canada, he led the company by offering innovative and specialized IT infrastructure, support, and advisory services in the areas of private equity, hedge, and family offices. The firm offered services such as IP Telephony, video conferencing, structured cabling, advanced secure IP networks, cyber security policies and framework enablement, and virtual CIO. He also is actively involved in helping clients with investors' due diligence in the advisory board panel participation. Some projects he worked includes merger and acquisition with Mercer Consulting, based in New York, and IT audit with Deloitte and KPMG here in Toronto.

Go to https://adaptandovercomebook.deskflix.com to find out on how FORTIFY + 1 works in the new world.

You can reach also Chee Lam at clam@deskflix.com or connect him at https://www.linkedin.com/in/cheelam.

What Employees Need to Know About Securely Working Remotely

By Izak Oosthuizen

Unplanned Overnight Remote Working – a Perfect Storm

The worldwide pandemic caused many businesses' employees to work remotely from home literally with no notice and not enough time for a thorough remote working security assessment.

Businesses have sent millions of employees to work remotely "unarmed" and vulnerable. Generally, home networks are unsecure, devices are shared for personal use, and Wi-Fi can be overwhelmed with VPN traffic. Residential internet service is not, by design, made for an entire work force to work from home because of limited bandwidth. Furthermore, business VPNs have overloaded many systems that had not been tested and ready for everyone to work from home.

> *"Cybercriminals have been given a golden oppor-*
> *tunity to take advantage of the global COVID-19*
> *pandemic to launch attacks on people working*
> *from home, as companies try their utmost to keep*
> *their organizations operational."*
>
> *-Bryan Hamman, regional director at Netscout[23]*

A perfect storm lies ahead. We now need to ensure we are properly equipped.

The Reality

Almost 2000 new coronavirus-related domains have been registered since the end of April, 2020, and 17% of those are malicious or suspicious.[24] Impersonating popular video conferencing apps like Zoom and Microsoft Teams is a popular choice for cybercriminals, often using phishing to get the victim to click on a link that either delivers malware or that tricks the user into revealing sensitive information.

About 230 Pasco County parents tuned in to a Zoom meeting on the evening of June 11, 2020, to hear the school superintendent Kurt Browning talk about plans to return to campus in August. Suddenly, a stream of new participants poured into

---

[23] https://www.bizcommunity.com/Article/196/661/203954.html
[24] https://www.engineeringnews.co.za/article/it-professionals-report-increased-cybersecurity-threats-related-to-remote-working-2020-05-26/rep_id:4136

the call, which organizer Denise Nicholas said was supposed to be on a paid secure version of Zoom. The uninvited "guests" weren't interested in whether Pasco County schools would be using a split day schedule or online education. Instead, they spouted racist rantings while taking over the screen with pornographic images. Nicholas quickly shut the meeting down and reported the incident to Zoom.[25]

The type of incident is called Zoom bombing, and it's been occurring more and more as public meetings have moved online during the pandemic. The problem is that the impact on business can lead to hefty fines for any sensitive data breaches and data loss, but there also is irreparable reputation damage – one out of five businesses is forced to close after a cyberattack.[26]

The remote workforce needs help because of the very open and real threat.

"Over one third of businesses experienced a security incident with a remote employee's action." OpenVPN[27]

[25] https://www.tampabay.com/news/pasco/2020/06/11/pasco-pta-zoom-meeting-gets-hacked-with-porn-racist-rants/
[26]https://www.computerweekly.com/news/450301845/One-in-five-businesses-hit-by-ransomware-are-forced-to-close-study-shows
[27] https://openvpn.net/remote-workforce-cybersecurity-quick-poll/

Immediate "Must-Take Steps" We Need to Execute

How do we keep ourselves secure when working remotely, especially because for many us this is the first time?

Attacks are occurring across a range of channels – cloud, cell phone, and the e-commerce ecosystem. Organizations need a security solution that is robust and operates across channels if they hope to create the most secure possible experience for their staff, customers, and for sensitive data. Our employees have a responsibility, also, as follows:

- Be aware and train: attend any business-provided awareness training. If your organization does not have such training in place, you can still educate yourself. You should request formal awareness training from your manager.

- Follow your company IT policy: do not break the rules! Store documents on corporate structures, use the VPN, and do not use personal devices to access company data and emails. By all means, do not allow family to use your company-owned devices.

- Stay secure: use your company VPN when you are accessing the company network, especially when you are connecting from a public Wi-Fi.

- Relationship changes: let your manager know as soon as a relationship with a contractor or vendor changes, particularly one that you use that might have access to company systems.

- Implement home internet monitoring: there are many tools available to protect your home's internet with just a few simple and basic changes to your internet router – and some are free! This proactively will stop potentially dangerous ransomware and access to malicious websites from both personal and company devices.

- Keep home devices updated: always ensure you have all home devices updated with the latest security updates and have good quality anti-virus and malware software installed. This will prevent potential internal home network hijacks. Regular updates should cover cell phone devices and network routers.

- Change and enable passwords: ensure all devices have strong unique passwords to prevent unauthorized access – do not use your home internet router's default password for your WiFi.

- Random devices: do not connect unknown devices to your company-owned or even personal devices.

- Create a home IT policy: help and educate your family or housemates, agree to certain rules; for example, do not download or install illegal software or movies, which can lead to a home network slowdown, exploitation, and potentially great financial liability.

- Lock it: Always ensure you lock your company-owned devices when you are taking a break or otherwise away from your workspace.

- Backup: always ensure you have at least one backup for photos and files on your personal devices – or two! Do not assume if you are using a cloud storage system that it provides backups.

"More than 40% of reported security breaches are caused by employee negligence." Research shows that employees are often the root cause of business security breaches. More training will help, but better security will require cultural change.[28]

Using Cloud Storage to Backup Personal Files

Online storage that allows you to store photos, videos, and files – accessible through the web or app – is owned by someone else, "the provider." There are a few known and trusted providers that offer some storage at no charge or for a minimal fee, as illustrated in the following chart:

---

[28]https://www.techrepublic.com/article/over-40-of-reported-security-breaches-are-caused-by-employee-negligence/

PROVIDER	FREE STORAGE	50GB	100GB	200GB	1TB
Google Drive	15GB		$1.99	$2.99	$9.99
Box	10GB		$17.30		
OneDrive	5GB		$59.99		
Apple iCloud	5GB	$0.99		$2.99	$9.99
Amazon Drive	5GB		$11.99		$59.99
Dropbox	2GB				$19.99
Flickr	1,000 photos (any resolution)				

Price as of 22 June 2020 in United States

How much storage do I need? The average per mobile phone has +/- 50 GB for photos, videos, and other files. How many cell phones do you have? Another good indicator is that 2 GB gives you enough space for 1,000 images, 20,000 documents, or five minutes of HD video. The more files you have, the more storage you need.

Tips to keep your personal data safe in cloud storage:

- Always ensure you have another backup in the event of failure

- Change your password regularly

- Do not use predictable passwords

- Enable two-step authentications, whenever possible. This is also known as two-factor authentication.

- Disable auto uploads for sensitive data

- Ensure you accept updates at every opportunity

Do not use this for busines data. Note: If you are an Amazon prime member, you get unlimited space.

Top Online Scams Related to the Current Pandemic

Criminals are devious opportunists who will use fearmongering related to local or global disasters to take advantage of people. Currently they are using the COVID-19 pandemic as the basis to prey on everyone possible – do not fret and allow it to overwhelm you into making mistakes. Some commonly known scams you need to look out for are:

- Fake websites
- Bogus medical equipment
- Deceitful miracle cures, vaccines, and treatments
- Expedited stimulus checks
- "Government-issued" online coronavirus tests
- Fake small business loans
- Donation scams

They normally use various social media channels to get you to engage and will, from time to time, claim to be local government officials.

"Coronavirus-related scams have cost Americans $13.4 million so far this year" reported by the Federal Trade Commission[29]

Google blocks over 18 million phishing emails related to coronavirus on a daily basis.[30] Scammers' websites pose as the real thing, collecting personal data and credit card numbers. With over 40,000 domain names using the word "coronavirus," you have to be on alert.

Phishing Tips – Stop the Tricks!

Remote workers faced a barrage of over 100,000 phishing attacks within four months, mostly involving Google-branded websites, according to a report by Barracuda Networks.[31] The phishing attacks applied a method known as spear phishing by impersonating legitimate websites to trick users into disclosing login credentials. Google-branded sites accounted for about 65,000 of the attacks, making up 65% of the attacks experienced during the study, while Microsoft-branded impersonation attacks accounted for just 13% of the attacks reported between January 1, 2020, and April 30, 2020.

---

[29]https://www.foxnews.com/tech/10-covid-19-scams-spreading-right-now-that-people-are-falling-for
[30]https://www.cpomagazine.com/cyber-security/google-blocks-over-18-million-daily-malware-and-phishing-emails-related-to-covid-19/
[31]https://www.cpomagazine.com/cyber-security/google-branded-phishing-attacks-account-for-65-of-threats-facing-remote-workers/#:~:text=Remote%20workers%20faced%20a%20barrage,credentials%20by%20impersonating%20legitimate%20websites.

"75% of all attacked business reported fraudulent emails."[32]

Phishing scams may be unsophisticated and annoying, but their frequency makes them a matter of concern. Phishing emails are the most common attack used by cybercriminals, and the risks and opportunities increase when working remotely.

Teach Your Employees to Look Out For the Following Types of Emails:

- Sent from a suspicious sender's email address

- Suspicious and unexpected attachments from known and unknown senders

- Request to confirm personal and financial information

- Poor grammar and spelling mistakes

- Aggressive, demanding, and threatening language – do not panic!

- Request to click "here," even if it looks like it is from a legitimate sender or vendor

- Request to change your password (but first to confirm your credentials)

---

[32] https://www.itgovernance.co.uk/blog/75-of-organisations-have-been-hit-by-spear-phishing

Remote Working Success Tips – Keep Us All Stable

Working remotely has many benefits. Beyond cybersecurity risks, however, we need to help staff stay focused and contribute to your business' success. Here are a few simple tips for your staff to break the monotony of working from home:

- Frequent breaks: set yourself a timer for breaks – coffee break, exercise, lunch. Breaks mean leaving your cell phone at your desk. Take a break and turn off your work.

- Stick to your plan: have fixed start and finish times

- Keep it professional: you are at work, get your mindset right, do not break your work routine, set your alarm to wake at the same time, shower, get dressed – do not work in your pajamas.

- Your desk and setup: ensure you have dedicated work space separate from home

- Focus: there are many distractions at home and proactive planning can help with potential interruptions, whether it is locking the door, or improving your lighting

- Stay in touch: connect with co-workers, set up regularly scheduled check-ins, and break the isolation

- Agreed expectations: Know what your company's expectations are. Communicate and report your concerns and questions to your manager.

> *"Security organizations must ensure existing protections and capabilities function in a newly remote environment, that users are aware of the threats and how to identify them and that organizations have implemented security best practices for remote work."*

> *Cisco Threat Intelligence team[33]*

The reality is that cyberattacks will continue to grow, and organizations will have to look at radically strengthening their cyber defenses around a critical infrastructure. However, implementing these controls and measures will go a long way to helping businesses keep their remote workforce safe. We need to continue to educate ourselves and stay aware.

---

[33] https://blogs.cisco.com/security/talos/threat-update-covid-19

About the Author

Izak Oosthuizen,

Zhero Founder & MD, London EO Member

Izak Oosthuizen has over 20+ years of experience in numerous IT functions from an operational perspective with strong focus on risk mitigation and cybersecurity. He has worked and collaborated with the likes of UK Space Agency, WeWork, Energy UK, Edmond De Rothschild, Federation of Master Builders and Dimension Data.

Zhero is a Microsoft Gold partner providing tailored risk mitigation, cybersecurity, cloud, business IT support, consultancy, and professional services to a range of industry sectors including finance, legal, insurance, architecture and advertising.

Izak pioneered the "Zhero Cloud", a practical, secure and all-in-one solution for SME's, available for a fraction of the costs compared to other public offerings. As part of the "Zhero Cloud" solution customers in architecture, video, and advertising get a unique, fast serverless system.

Izak is also a member of the Entrepreneurs Organisation London and has a passion to help people experience the transformative power of IT with strong focus on risk mitigation and cyber security. He has a ground-breaking 99% client retention over the past 10 years.

Are you concerned about security? Book a strategy call with Izak here:
https://calendly.com/izakoosthuizen/30